THE SHAPES OF

OUR SINGING

THE SHAPES OF

OUR SINGING

A GUIDE TO THE METRES AND SET FORMS
OF VERSE FROM AROUND THE WORLD

by

Robin Skelton

EASTERN WASHINGTON UNIVERSITY PRESS
SPOKANE, WASHINGTON

Cover and book design by Scott Poole

Library of Congress Cataloging-in-Publication Data

Skelton, Robin —
        The Shapes of our singing: a comprehensive guide to verse
forms and metres from around the world / by Robin Skelton
                p. cm. -
ISBN 0-910055-76-9 (pbk.)
        I. Title

PN1031.S68165 2001
808.1—dc21
                                2001040665

For all those who helped this book come into being,
and for all those who will read it.

CONTENTS

FRENCH

GERMAN

RUSSIAN

SANSKRIT

SPANISH

YIDDISH

INTRODUCTION

I. THE SELECTION

No one book could describe and give examples of all the set forms and metres in the world. This is, therefore, a selection and the principles I have followed in making my selection are :

Firstly, I have presented no set form or metre that has not been used by several writers over a long period, or is not commonly regarded as a traditional form in folk verse. There are a few exceptions to this rule. These were chosen in order to awaken interest in a little known form of a language not commonly regarded as significant in the history of verse, or largely forgotten. I instance Breton, Catalan, Cornish, Ethiopian, Vietnamese. I have also taken the liberty of including examples of three forms of my own invention, *Catena Rondo, Viator, and Novem.*

Secondly, I have attempted to present a complete account of the forms and metres of English and of French, Spanish, Italian, Welsh, and Irish. I have also given a complete account of the set forms of China and Japan. This has been possible because the forms and metres of these languages are clearly defined with established formulae.

Thirdly, I have made shorter selections from those languages in which a very large number of metres exist, but are all variations upon or elaborations upon a series of "key" patterns. Consequently, I have presented six Sanskrit metres of the five hundred or so in existence, and only eight of the almost equally numerous Arabic metres. There are supposedly over one hundred and fifty Skaldic metres; I have given four of them alongside four Eddic metres in the section devoted to Old Norse.

Fourthly, I have presented every known Classical metre, including several that were only used very rarely or as part of other metres. Greek verse (which, with some few exceptions also means Latin verse) is at the root of so much later work in other languages that I felt it should be fully represented.

Fifthly, I have tackled the difficult problem of deciding which language owns which particular form by deciding, on the whole, that the form or metre belongs to the language that either perfected it or made the greatest use of it. Thus many forms originating in Provence are not labelled Provencal (or Occitan) but French or Italian. The Pantoum, which originated in Malaya, is listed as French. The various kinds of sonnet are scattered between Italian and English, though, in fact, the Sonnet was common in most European languages.

Finally, I have allowed myself some liberties. I have given a small number of forms more than one illustration because one example did not do them justice. I have also included variations which might offend a purist.

I have not explored in this book, the various varieties of rhyme as rhyme operates quite differently in different languages. One man's consonance, one might say, is another man's rhyme. Without a great deal of phonetic exploration the different uses of rhyme could not be handled.

I regret very much the absence of some languages whose forms and metres appear to have remained unrecorded, or recorded only as songs; it is almost impossible to translate song rhythms into metre if the language itself is strange to the ear, and while there are some repeated tunes in all cultures, they are rarely absolutely identical with each other. Because of these difficulties many languages are not represented here. In addition, it must be recognized that much poetry is written in free verse and therefore is not relevant to this volume. A large number of countries have moved from oral to printed literature in the last half century and the poetry that has emerged is largely in non-metrical verse. This is, in its way, ironic, for the set forms and metres of poetry originated in oral performances, the definite shapes being mnemonic devices, and the sometimes contorted metrical ingenuities an admired aspect of the speaker/singer's court entertainers; the new poetry of developing countries is addressed to a different audience and readership.

II. THE APPROACH

There are several ways of making use of the verse forms and metres of languages other than one's own. One method is that of numerous composers of Haiku in English; they not only follow the syllable count precisely but also obey the rules about content which have been established by long tradition. They create a kind of pastiche. The results are often very subtle and penetrating. On the other hand, however, these Haiku are more imitations than creations; they do not move onward from their beginnings.

One may contrast this approach with that of the poets of the Renaissance in England. They took the Italian sonnet form, replicated it quite exactly, and then reshaped it in a number of ways, providing us with the Shakespearean Sonnet and the Spenserian Sonnet. Later years produced the Miltonic Sonnet and numerous other variations. The proportions of the sonnet form were retained and, most usually, the line length; there was always a well shaped rhyme scheme. Some poems generally accepted as sonnets like Shelley's *Ozymandias* were not actually sonnets at all. The sonnet thus became a vehicle for many kinds of content; it developed a new and changing character.

It is, I believe, valuable to regard set forms and metres as opportunities for creating variations in this fashion. I have included three of my own invented forms as examples of this procedure; all three clearly derive from forms presented elsewhere in the book but differ from them in many ways.

The verse forms of Provence were not made subject to such experimentation for some time. When they became part of the French poetic tradition in the sixteenth century they were regularized and made subject to uniform rules. The Lai and Virelai, for example, became rigid forms rather than forms that permitted variation. Though this was so, the subject matter was less restricted; the attitudes of the troubadours were no longer wholly acceptable. Of course, the shift from Provencal to French is not as considerable as that from Italian to English, or Persian to English, as in Fitzgerald's *Rubaiyat of Omar Khayyam*. Fitzgerald's poem was a translation, but he did follow the verse shape of the original in his rhyming, though he shortened the lines of the quatrains, and formed a sequence of a gathering of poems made with no intention of forming any overall narrative. This is another way of dealing with foreign forms: follow the basic formal principles but adjust them to the cadences of ones own verse-speech, and utilize them in a fashion not intended, but not ruled out, by the original tradition. Fitzgerald did not use the original metre of the Persian.

Only a small number of ingenious writers have attempted to replicate the sounds of the original verse forms, Pound and Zukovsky being two of them. Unfortunately, this approach can never work except, perhaps, as a teaching device. Some of the sounds made in other languages than one's own are almost impossible to utilize. How would one put the xhosa 'click' into a poem, or make use of the Welsh "ll"?

A further problem occurs when one considers the rhythm of verse. While English and most modern European languages organize their metres in terms of stressed and unstressed syllables, other languages arrange their patterns in terms of "long" and "short" syllables, the length of each syllable being determined by rules peculiar to the languages involved. Attempts have been made to write this "quantitative" verse in English, but they have not been successful as metrical constructs, though some of them, for example by Tennyson, have turned out to be good poems. The solution to this problem is to recreate long syllables as accented ones and short syllables as unaccented and this has been the general practice since the eighteenth century when the German poet, F.G. Klopstock, established the method.

In making my own poems in the forms and metres of other languages I have changed quantitative into accentual metres. I have followed the syllable counts exactly. I have also followed the rhyme schemes exactly, but from time to time have substituted English rhyming practices for foreign ones. Some rhyming in foreign languages would be considered assonance or consonance in English; on those occasions I have used the less emphatic sounds.

In the matter of content I have followed two differing principles. Firstly, I have been concerned to see if I could make a certain form function effectively in English, not only with English locutions, but with imagery that is natural to English, or western, culture. Secondly, I have, in a number of poems, accepted the traditional views of the content appropriate to particular forms to see if these limitations can be effective in a different language. I have done my best to respect my sources and have avoided mere ingenuity or frivolity on almost all occasions. I have also, and deliberately, made a number of poems that echo each other by being concerned with the same themes. These are the traditional ones that have been at the heart of poetry for centuries: the seasons, dawn, evening, love (of course) and death. Each form produces a different tone and, therefore, a different message, and thus additional light is shed upon the relationship between form and content in regulated verse.

III. TERMINOLOGY

I have chosen to use as little of the special vocabulary of academic prosody as possible, and when I have used a particular term I have explained it. Nevertheless, no English book dealing with verse can avoid using the metrical categories of classical Greek and Latin. Here, therefore, is a complete list of the classical groups of syllables known as feet, which are also used in describing verse in English and other modern European languages.

FEET OF TWO SYLLABLES

Iamb	˘ ʹ	before, alone, despair
Trochee	ʹ ˘	gently, venture, over
Spondee	ʹ ʹ	Dodo, hatrack, flywheel
Pyrrhic	˘ ˘	in the, at a, of a

FEET OF THREE SYLLABLES

Amphibrach	˘ ʹ ˘	Denoted, remotely, attending, division
Amphimacer or Cretic	ʹ ˘ ʹ	outermost, peregrine, dragoman
Anapaest	˘ ˘ ʹ	the canoe, to betray

Dactyl	′ ⌣ ⌣	hurriedly, bargaining, wanderer
Molossus	′ ′ ′	big bad wolf, ding dong bell
Tribrach	⌣ ⌣ ⌣	into the, and as if
Bacchic	′ ′ ⌣	rolled over, old woman
Anti-Bacchic	⌣ ′ ′	an old man, a lone wolf

FEET OF FOUR SYLLABLES

Antispast	⌣ ′ ′ ⌣	the vast darkness, a strange vision
Choriamb	′ ⌣ ⌣ ′	cold and alone, clearly aware
Di-iamb	⌣ ′ ⌣ ′	alone again, before the mast
Di-trochee	′ ⌣ ′ ⌣	lonely darkness, future trouble
Epitrite	⌣ ′ ′ ′	a big bad wolf
	′ ⌣ ′ ′	hit a bad wolf
	′ ′ ⌣ ′	bad wolf destroyed
	′ ′ ′ ⌣	bad wolf ended
Ionic a majore	′ ′ ⌣ ⌣	lone wanderer
Ionic a minore	⌣ ⌣ ′ ′	the betrayed girl
Paeon	′ ⌣ ⌣ ⌣	Dimly in a, Singing of a,
	⌣ ′ ⌣ ⌣	a wanderer
	⌣ ⌣ ′ ⌣	in the morning
	⌣ ⌣ ⌣ ′	into the dark
Proceleusmatic	⌣ ⌣ ⌣ ⌣	at an undis-, in and of the,

Classical metres are formed of syllables regarded as "long" or "short" according to a system of rules that cannot be made to apply in English verse where the syllables are grouped together according to the amount of emphasis (of accent, or stress) given them. Classical feet are given accentual-syllabic form in English, as in the examples above. As I have already said, this has been a general practice since this solution to the problem was discovered in the eighteenth Century. So called Quantitative verse therefore becomes Accentual-Syllabic.

Some metres ignore patterns of long and short, accented and unaccented syllables, and are based entirely upon the actual syllable count. This is so with Chinese, Japanese, Welsh and Irish verse.

A further kind of metre pays no attention to anything other than the number of accented syllables; there can be as many unaccented ones as the writer wishes. This, called by Gerard Manley Hopkins "Sprung Verse," is also called Podic Verse, and was far from original with Hopkins. In English poetry it can be found in the work of John Skelton (1460-1529).

It has been necessary to use some few special terms in many of these entries. These are:

Assonance which means a repetition of vowel sounds rather than of vowel and consonant combinations, as in heed, feet.

Consonance which means a repetition of consonants, as in dust, bed. If the consonantal repetitions follow each other closely and form the beginnings of words, then we have *Alliteration*, as in dust, dead.

Caesura means a break in the line of verse, usually near the middle, though Caesura may occur more than once. The break should be a natural breath pause, or a pause to give the reader a moment of anticipation before an important word.

Substitution occurs when one foot in the regular metrical pattern is replaced by a different foot.

In presenting the metrical patterns, I have indicated a stressed or accented syllable with the mark ´ , an unaccented one with the mark ˇ , and one which may be either stressed or unstressed and which is termed an *ancept* with the mark - . Only very occasionally do the metrical rules demand that a syllable be partly stressed, and when this occurs I have used the mark ½. Usually partially stressed syllables are accepted as being legitimate modulations of the set feet, and scanned as either stressed or unstressed in order to fit with the given metre.

Metres may be described in terms of the number of feet the lines contain, thus a one-foot line would be a monometer, a two-foot line a dimeter, and, after that, a trimeter (3), a tetrameter (4), a pentameter (5), a hexameter (6), and a heptameter (7). These terms are generally used only to describe English and European metres.

IV. SOURCES AND ACKNOWLEDGMENTS

I have taken my information on set forms and metres from many published works. In general, I am most indebted to the 1974 Enlarged Edition of the *Princeton Encyclopedia of Poetry and Poetics* and its successor, *The New Princeton Encyclopedia of Poetry* and Poetics of 1993, both published by Princeton University Press. I also owe something to Lewis Turco's, *The New Book of Forms*, (University Press of New England, 1986), and have adopted some of his suggestions. I owe a considerable debt, as must any writer on English versions of French forms, to Gleeson White's critical anthology of 1887, *Ballades and Rondeaus, Chants Royal, Sestinas, Villanelles and Co.* Among the other general works I have consulted, in which I have taken particular pleasure, are George Saintsbury's *Historical Manual of English Prosody* of 1910, Babette Deutch's Poetry Handbook, *A Dictionary of Terms*, (1957) and the anthology, *Strong Measures: Contemporary American Poetry in Traditional Forms*, compiled by Philip Dacey and David Jauss (Harper & Row, 1986).

Many other books have been of use and three of them deserve special mention. I could not have produced my section on Irish forms without Gerard Murphy's *Early Irish Lyrics*, (Clarendon Press, 1956) and my Welsh section would have been impossible without the work of Gwyn Williams in his, *An Introduction to Welsh Poetry*, (Faber & Faber, 1953) and also the example of Rolfe Humphries in his collection of poems in Welsh Forms, *Green Armor on Green*

Ground, (1956) which was included in his *Collected Poems of 1965*, (Indiana University Press). Lee M. Hollander helped me a great deal with his, *The Skalds*, (University of Michigan Press, 1968); other specialized works I have mentioned in the text.

A number of these poems have already appeared in print. The Irish section was published by Salmon Publishing in Ireland under the title *Samhain*, and the Welsh section appeared under the imprint of, The Old Stile Press in Wales with the title, *Inheritance*. All but four of the poems in the Japanese section were included in my collection of poems in Japanese forms, *Islands*, published by the Ekstasis Press in Canada. Approximately half of the poems in the "Classical Metres" section appeared as a chapbook, *A Formal Music,* published for the Hawthorne Society by Reference West also in Canada.

Some poems have been taken from earlier books of mine. *Collected Shorter Poems, 1947-1977*, (Sono Nis,1981), contained "The Mark," "A Ballad of Despair," "The Hearing," and "The Farewell." "That Evening," "Love's Wisdom" and "On the Mountain" were included in *Because of Love*, (McClelland and Stewart, 1977). *Popping Fuchsias,* (Cacanadadada, 1992) included "Narcissist," "Carol for Yule," and "In the Hospice." Some poems have been included in anthologies: "Love in an English Garden" in *A Burning Candle*, (Poetry Now, 1993), "October Again" in *The Clayoquot Diary 1994,* (The Clayoquot Resource Centre, 1993), "Wood in August" in *Clear-Cut Words, Writers for Clayoquot*, (Reference West for the Hawthorne Society, 1993), and "Night Blossom in April" and "The Cavern" in *The Studio Cafe Anthology*, (Calgary, 1993).

Other poems have appeared in the Canadian periodicals *Arc, The Unfettered Mind, Poetry Newsletter, Magical Arts*, and in *Nimrod* (U.S.A.), *Oasis* and *Literary Review* (U.K.). I am grateful to the editors and publishers concerned for their support and for permission to reprint these poems.

I am also immensely grateful to a number of people who have helped in the making of this book in several ways. Firstly, I must thank Jocelyn Bates, who made sense of a confusing manuscript and provided me with a functioning disc and readable text. The text itself owes a great deal to the critical acumen and editorial skills of Margaret Blackwood, Anne Kelly and Kerry Slavens, who saved many poems from disaster. Much needed information was provided in books loaned to me by Mary Clark, Rhonda Batchelor, and Charles Lillard. I must add that without the constant support and the editorial help of my wife Sylvia, this book, like its predecessors, would never have been made and it is to her companionship and to the financial support of the Canada Council that I owe those poems deriving from travels in Italy and Greece. No book is ever the work of only one man.

Robin Skelton
Victoria, B.C.
Canada

THE SHAPES OF

OUR SINGING

ANGLO - SAXON

The Love Song

Venturing on vision, avoiding men's voices,
planning a poetry to make all plain,
loosening love from the laws of logic
granting it greater goodness in song,
I find I am framing my thoughts in a fashion
long-lost and alien to today's language,
yet somehow the sense of it, tense in each sentence,
registers rhythms, riding rough-shod
over the versecraft of today's talkers,
drumbeats of dancers, words in the wind —
or am I mistaken, mimicking manners
of old forefathers whose fevers and furies
are lost or in limbo?
                              I bring long ago
back as I brood on the beauty I try for
and find that the faces of love are not different,
the songs much the same for all the odd accents;
love remains love and the lovers are dancing.

Alliterative verse in Old German and Anglo-Saxon consisted basically of lines in which two stressed syllables in the first half line alliterated with one or more syllables in the second half. Though much alliterative verse is rhythmical there is no requirement about metre, the only consideration being the number of stressed syllables. These should be made the basis of the verse, each line having the same number of stresses, or the same number with occasional variations. The most usual length of line is between four and six stresses. The Alliterative metre is also to be found in the poetry of Scandinavia.

STRICT ALLITERATIVE VERSE I

Relaxed

During days of dreaming under
stainless skies, the summer steady,
making music, man's immortal.

In the 1880s, the scholar Eduard Sievers divided alliterative verse into five types. These types were not to be seen as forming consistent patterns within one passage of verse; they were mingled. Nevertheless, the types do exist and can be regarded as forming set metres. This example is Sievers A; each half line, or hemistich, has two stresses and the rhythm runs ´˘ ´˘, the stressed syllables alliterating.

STRICT ALLITERATIVE VERSE II

The Start of Spring

When song asserts the start of Spring
and dances dazzle dawn each day,
perceptive poets prepare for pain.

This verse is in the pattern Sievers called Type B. The rhythm is ⌣′ ⌣′ ⌣′ ⌣′, the stressed syllables being alliterated.

In Grief

My heart holding you hopelessly
in dream's darkness, your dear presence
remakes moonlight, reminds mourning
that lives linger, have long stories.

This verse is in the Sievers Type C pattern, in which the third syllable of the half line is only very lightly stressed, the rhythm of the half line running ⌣′ ½⌣, the ½ standing for a light or secondary stress.

November Ending

Loose leaves drift the lawn's long smoothness;
Time's tune alters; tall tress waver
slate sky shines through stripped bare branches
fine frost-fingers fur dawn's windows.

This verse is in the pattern Sievers regarded as the fourth type. The third syllable in the half line is only partially stressed and indicated by ½. The complete line runs: ′ ′ ½⌣ * ′ ′ ½⌣.

News Item

Word-wise, I hear war warnings fill
men's mouths and know man means to kill;
we wait the way wild creatures wait,
keep close our fear, control our pride.

This is the fifth type of alliterative verse as described by Sievers.
The rhythm of the full line runs: ◠ ½ ˇ ◠ * ◠ ½ ˇ ◠ .

ARABIC

Thorn Trees

Beneath cold skies
   the crouched thorn trees
      are small dark gods;
they own strong spells,
   if torn down curse
      the heart, hand, mind;
when spring comes round
   their soft spread petals
      bless love's games;
the old ones swear
   their moonlit dancing
      sends men blind.

The Hazaj metre is composed in half lines (or hemistiches) of 12 syllables divided into three parts, the rhythm of each half line being ⌣ ╱ ╱   ⌣ ╱ ╱   ⌣ ╱ ╱.

In Arabic prosody, the sequence of rhythmic units, which I will term feet, is laid down but the starting point in the sequence may alter. When this occurs, the metre is given another name. Thus the sequence used for the Hajaz metre could be rearranged to begin with ╱ ╱ ⌣ and would then be the Rajaz metre; if it began with ╱ ╱ ⌣ ╱ it would be the Ramal metre.

The above poem is a conventional rhymed couplet. I have given each hemistich a three step form to emphasize the shape of the whole.

Leaf Dance

In fall days the dry leaves alarm air with swift flight,
despair spinning death's dancers, grief twisting day's
      light,
but each death renews birth as earth welcomes time past
and feeds seed as men feed the fresh dawn with old
      night.

The Mutaqarib metre is composed in lines of 24 syllables divided into two half lines, or hemistiches, of 12 syllables each with the rhythm ⌄⁄⁄ ⌄⁄⁄ ⌄⁄⁄ ⌄⁄⁄. In the above verse, I have indented the second hemistich of each of the two lines which form a couplet of the kind that opens the Ghasel and in which the first two hemistiches rhyme, that rhyme being then made the end rhyme for the following full line or lines.

QSIDAH IN THE BASIT METRE

Sandstorm

Sand blinds the sun, swathing day.
  Half darkness grows almost night;
breath gasps and eyes, clogged, inflamed,
  lids swollen, wince back from light.

Pain rakes the skin; trapped, we hide;
  cool caverns, deep wells allow
strained lungs to breathe, fear again

storm dance, the earth's desert rite.

A Qasidah is composed in lines of 28 syllables divided into two
hemistiches of 14 syllables each. The first two hemistiches rhyme
and the same rhyme ends the following full line or lines.

    The Basit metre has eight feet in the line, each half line having
the rhythm ´´˘´ ´˘´ ´´˘´ ´˘´. This rhythmical sequence is
also used for the Tawil and Madid metres.

    In the above example, I have indented the second half of each
hemistich so that each stanza, in fact, forms one complete line.

RAJAZ METRE

Aftermath

Dawn holds its breath
    till, over trees,
       light fills the sky.
Leaves tremble, shake;
    dew slides from grass;
       cloud slithers by.

Love stirs in bed,
    sheets find the floor,
       soft slippers grip
smooth feet, and eyes
    blur watchful glass;
       tears taste the lie.

The Rajaz metre is composed in half lines (hemistiches) of 12 syllables divided into three parts, the rhythm being: ´´˘´ * ´´˘´
* ´´˘´.

    Each verse is a couplet which may or may not rhyme.

In the above, the hemistiches are arranged in a three step manner to emphasize the form.

Sea Coast

Tides sift the sand,
   shift pebbles, rocks;
      seaweed tangles;
waves' claws expose
   grey fossil wheels,
      time still turning;
brown boulder clay
   slides wetly, shines;
      high tides ravage.
Long year on year
   sea's raped this land:
      Earth, take warning.

The Sari Metre is composed in half lines of 12 syllables divided into three parts, the rhythm of each half line being ´ ´ ˘ ´ ´ ´ ˘ ´ ´ ´ ˘ . Other metres using the same rhythmic sequence are the Munsarih, Khafif, Mudari, Muqtadab, and Mujathth metres. The above example is a conventional rhyming couplet.

Entertainer

Her heels ring on cold hard boards;
  her silk skirt suggests bared thighs;
her eyes shine from black-rimmed lids;
  her red lips announce love's lies

in slow songs that hurt men's hearts
  with pain, shame, till drumbeats roll
their last chords. She smiles, bows, leaves
  the small stage that night-dreams prize.

The Tawil Metre is composed of 14 syllable hemistiches (or half lines) with the rhythm ⌣ ⁄ ⁄ ⌣ ⁄ ⁄ ⁄ ⌣ ⁄ ⁄ ⌣ ⁄ ⁄ ⁄. Other metres using the same rhythmic sequence are the Madid and Basit metres. These are in rhymed couplets as is common in Arabic verse.

This example is, in fact, one rhymed couplet, each stanza being one complete line of verse.

Myth

Hurled under tides' green darkness, he, hand shielding
    eyes,
  drifts slowly down red coral steeps, tells fishes lies,

shrewd, cunning, builds tall tales to please slow

swimming minds,
swears prophets say earth soon will end crass human
cries,

vows tidal truths found under moon's white light will stay
long after earth's burned crumbled dust, man's presence
gone.

He, trapped in tides' dream darkness, knows his day is
lost;
lies, truths and oaths mean nothing now: Love's burst
the sun.

Each Urjuzah is a series of rhyming couplets in the Rajaz metre which is composed in lines of 24 syllables divided into two hemistiches of 12 syllables each with the following rhythm: ´´˘´ ´´˘´ ´´˘´. In the above example, I have indented the second hemistich of each line and have treated each couplet as a separate stanza.

The rhythmical sequence used in the Rajaz metre is also that of the Hazaj and Ramal metres in Arabic.

Wafir Metre

The Remembered Ones

When I am alone
with memories' ghosts
I know I am old;
so many are here
beside me today
that shadows enfold

each word that I say,
  each name I recall,
    each face of my friends
that died or that left
  for places unknown,
    the heat or the cold,

but Time is absurd,
  itself a mere ghost,
    a shade of a shade
and leaves when the dawn
  of death that is life
    embraces our sight
and smiling returns
  the lost and the mourned
    that trouble the mind,
and all that has been
  is part of the day
    that clothes us in light.

The Wafir metre is composed in half lines of 15 syllables divided into three parts, each part having the rhythmic form ⌄ ⸍ ⌄ ⌄. Another metre using the same rhythmic sequence is the Kamil metre. The example above is in rhyming couplets, a common form in Arabic.

Each stanza is, in fact, a couplet, with the hemistiches arranged in a three step form.

BENGALI

Monsoon

When the rains come, beating down leaves
   breaking branches, drumming
the sun-scarred roofs, transfiguring
   roads and pathways, strumming
on each taut nerve their dark music,
   I bow my head and pray
that the great gods have mercy on
   the small lives of our day.

The Payar is a rhyming couplet and is found in Assamese and Oriya, as well as Bengali. Each line is made up of two halves, one of eight syllables and one of six, but the halves themselves are also divided by natural pauses, the first one into four and four syllables and the second into four and two. Each line could therefore be described as having the syllable count 4 4 * 4 2.

TRIPADI

Near Chakrata

Squatting beside the mountain track
stone supporting each ragged back
they held out brown hands bright with rough cut gems.

They had crossed the mountains from Tibet,
that endless mystery, to let
us have these jewels gouged from sacred streams.

Watching, I felt a kind of grief;
having lost all innocent belief,
I could not buy; suspicion stayed my hand.

Was their tale true? I do not know.
I've grieved for fifty years or so,
wishing I had been credulous and a fool.

The Tripadi is a form also to be found in Assamese and Oriya. It consists of two rhyming eight syllable lines followed by an un-rhymed ten syllable line. These "lines" are regarded as being parts of a line rather than lines themselves, but, in fact, the "line" would be regarded as a stanza in Western prosody, and I have treated it as such. Another form of the Tripadi has the line with a syllable count of 6 6 8, the two, six syllable lines rhyming with each other.

BRETON

By The Lake

As ripples bright with sunlight slide
across the lake's calm to make wide
and wider rings, and the wingbeat
of ravens high in the sky meet
reflected cloud with their proud spread,
thinking upon the long gone dead
I gaze deep down in the brown glass
and find absurd my blurred face,
this foolish mask I must ask still
to bear the shame of a tamed will.

Little Breton verse survives, but the fragments we have give us an
eight syllable line rhyming internally on the fourth and seventh
syllables and end-rhyming in couplets. This is a fourteenth century
structure.

B U R M E S E

Dreams

Trust in your dreams;
their night gleams know
what seems is true.

The Than-bauk is a three-line poem, conventionally an epigram,
each line being of four syllables, and the rhyme being on the fourth
syllable of the first line, the third syllable of the second one, and
the second one of the third. This has been called "climbing rhyme"
and is characteristic of Burmese verse.

YA-DU

In Winter

Air trembles now
and the bough shines,
the plough lies still
and the chill rain
stencils the window pane.

The role of the tree
is to be bare
to free air, keep

a dream's deep flow
in sleep till the green leaves grow.

Ya-du is the name for a short poem dealing usually with the seasons. It normally has three stanzas or fewer. The stanzas are of five lines, the first four being of four syllables and the fifth being longer and having 5, 7, 9 or 11 syllables. The rhyme scheme is complex. The rhyme in the first three lines is on the fourth, third, and second syllables. The third line ends with a syllable that rhymes with the third and second syllables of the two following lines. The fourth line ends with a word that rhymes with the last syllable of the stanza.

CATALAN

Garden Nightfall

The fading light
announces night
and shadows crawl
along the wall
of climbing vines
to form designs
of thrust and swerve,
each angle, curve
and twist absurd
with art, a word
and ideogram
that say 'I am
the final thought
that can't be bought
or even known
till day is done'.

This metre of four syllable couplets was used by Jaum Roig (d. 1478) in his *Llibre de les Dones*, rather than the eight syllable couplet usual in the period.

C H I N E S E

Alternatively

In the rock pool
    a blue sky
pins a white cloud
    on a shell,
or does the shell
    trap the cloud?
Am I the tongue
    or the bell?

Ch'i-yen-shih metre:
    Syllables: 7 7 7 7
    End rhymes: A B C B
Each line is composed of monosyllabic words and there is a caesura after the fourth word in each. In this example, I have indented the second part of each line.

M o o n t r u t h

For Michael Seward Snow

Full moon:
  a white light
carves shade;
  the warm night,
dream tamed,
  fears the dawn's
hard noise,
  the sun's bright

trees green
  not pearled grey,
walls grey
  not bleached white,
mind trapped
  as time's dream
feels time
  and takes flight.

The name Chueh-chu means, literally, "sonnet cut short" as Arthur Cooper pointed out in his translation of Li Po and Tu Fu. It consists of eight lines with the rhyme scheme A A B A C A D A or the rhyme scheme A B C B D B E B. A further variation is A A B A A A C A.

This example is in the Wu-yen-shih metre, which consists of five monosyllable lines with a caesura after the second syllable. Each syllable is a complete word.

P r a i r i e   S u m m e r

There's the vast blue
  of the sky
stretched far to far,
  so deep, high
it seems a dreamed
  and strange place,
and no man dares
  to ask why

high, why deep, why
  it should lie
in blue so pure
  man would die
to reach it, touch
  that great good,
share what makes all
  dry bones cry.

This "Chinese sonnet" is in the Ch'i-yen-shih metre.

S s u - Y e n - S h i h   M e t r e

S o n g

The hush   of rain
in the   ash tree

soft as the voice
of the far sea,

may tell me more
than man should know
of when and where
and to and fro.

Ssu-Yen-Shih Metre has quatrains composed of four monosyllable
lines with a caesura after the second word. The rhyme scheme is A
B C B.

Pools and Wells

Rain pools
  heed no dreams,
but wells,
  deep, reach far,
drink earth's
  chill dark streams,
tell us
  who we are.

Wu-Yen-Shih Metre has quatrains composed of four, five monosyllable lines with a caesura after the second word. The rhyme
scheme is A B A B.

CLASSICAL
GREEK & LATIN

Parthenon

Hunched on a rock slab,
clasping her raised knees,
dressed as if mourning
here on this great mount
named for Athena,
guarding her city,
scorning the crowded
tourists, she offers
nothing but sadness,
watches a dark sea
tilt the horizon,
dreams of the islands
rubbled with temples,
thinks of the music
lost to our fingers.

Wisdom befriends me
seeing her seated
there on the rock slab
darkly unmoving
sending this message
whether she means to
send it or only
rests in the sunlight.

The Adonic foot has the rhythmic form ´ ˘ ˘ ´ ´ or ´ ˘ ˘ ´ ˘.

The Garden at Dawn

The frost is bright as glass in the chill of dawn;
the cherry tree is black to the lucent sky;
I take a step towards the woodshed,
feeling it changed to a throbbing cavern.

My morning mind is clouded and blurred with dream;
dream holds the one great key to the shining whole
we share with whirlpools, gods, and children
aware realities move like music,

slow, deep, or quick, light, dancing and keeping time
with earth and sky, eternity felt in tune
for moments only, shaping moments,
changing the shed to a holy darkness.

And yet a question troubles me; shed and cave
are surely something other than false or true?
Clouds move across dawn skies and boughs curve.
Time has a different colder question:

Soon death will end sight, light, and the music heard
in waking, dreaming, pondering; all will go.
Go where? The dark shed, cave, or tomb knows;
so does the vanishing frost, the great tree.

Alcaics are composed in four line stanzas. The first line is metri-

cally ´ ´ ˘ ´ ´ ´ ˘ ˘ ´ ˘ ´ , but the first and second feet may be
changed to ˘ ´ ˘ and ´ ˘ ´ and the last foot to ˘ ´ . The second
line has the same rhythm as the first with or without variation. The
third line is metrically ´ ´ ˘ ´ ´ ´ ˘ ´ ´ , but all the feet may be
changed and become ˘ ´ ˘ ´ ˘ ´ ˘ ´ ˘ , not necessarily as a whole;
individual feet may be changed by themselves. The fourth line is
´ ˘ ˘ ´ ˘ ˘ ´ ˘ ´ ´ , but the last foot may be changed to ´ ˘ . Both
Swinburne and Tennyson composed poems in Alcaics.

Alcmanic Metre

Invocation

Rapt and at peace with the pillars of stone
lifting their phalluses tall to the sky,
praising the goddess of miriad names,
she of the mountain, the woodland, the field,
kneeling I tell her our need of her strength,
mercy, compassion; the tribes are at war,
burning the houses, the orchards, the vines,
muddying her springs and her echoing wells,
raping the women that mirror her smile,
spitting the children on lances and knives.
Goddess return, for religion has died;
temples are empty and laws are abused.
Goddess return to us, answer our call,
bring us the good of your mothering hands.

The Alcmanic metre is formed of ten syllable lines with the rhythm:
´ ˘ ˘ ´ ˘ ˘ ´ ˘ ˘ ´ ´ . It could also be described as either dactylic
trimeter hypercatalectic, which is to say three dactyls (´ ˘ ˘) with
an extra half or whole foot, or dactylic tetrameter catalectic, which
consists of four dactyls, the last one being incomplete. Alcman

moved away from the dactylic hexameter and created a number of shorter lined and more lyrical metres.

Island of Wine

An island was labelled Calliste
then Thera, but names do not matter;
its people felt warnings, departed
before the volcanic eruption,
the splitting of earth, but accepted
the duties their birth laid upon them,
returned to the island, rebuilding,
reshaping, from lava and ashes.

The names do not matter; the story
is loyalty, faith and survival,
persistence, discovery, beauty,
an island of vines, Santorini,
the dew on the grapes of the morning,
the song of the wine and its radiance
announcing a truth of creation.

This earth is a woman in labour;
her children are born of upheavals,
renewals, destructions of mountains,
of oceans and forests and rivers;
her throes are the makers of islands.
Respect her and care for her creatures;
protect her, give thanks for her riches,
and wine will be granted the spirit,
the body, the mind, and our children.

The Amphibrach is a metrical foot with the rhythm ˘ ´ ˘. Lines composed wholly of amphibrachs are rare in both Greek and Latin.

Anacreontics

Athens

In the air of Athens clogged thick
with the fumes of traffic, trees smeared
by the settling grime, I breathed deep
a divine and ageless wild scent,
and, enraptured, heard a plucked string
and a voice that sang a far song,
and I grieved, ashamed of bad verse
as the tuneless traffic beat drums.

The Anacreontic metre is composed of eight syllable lines running: ˘˘´ ˘˘´ ´´. The last syllable may sometimes be short (or unstressed); when this occurs, the metre resembles that of the Finnish.

Anapaestic Dimeter

The Dance

In the hour of the dawn
I recover a tune
that reminds me of dance,
of a measure I've known

as a movement of light
in the mind of the earth
and the steps are the steps
of both maidens and gods
in the circles of stone
that are cupped by the hills
with a canopy sky.

In the hills of the dawn
I perceive that the tune
I have said I recall
is as new as the grass
interspersing the stones
of the pavement I tread
not remembered at all
but a gift, a surprise
from the spirit of things,
yet it motions my feet
in familiar ways.

In the temple of dawn
I am shuffling a step
that is older than dawn
or the order of time.
I am dancing the stars
that are farther than stars.
I am part of the song.

The Anapaestic dimeter has the rhythmic pattern ⏑ ⏑ ⁄ ⏑ ⏑ ⁄ .

Artemis

Her face marble, I hear Webster,
Mine eyes dazzle; she died young,
but earth's goddess denies dying,
retains youth as a true beauty
retains grace, her defined bones
a shaped wonder, a clear music,
her eyes dazzling the awed stranger.
We count centuries, maintain *Ancient,*
Before Christ, but a world spirit
is poised here, a bright goddess
of proud laughters and strange glory,
a young woman, a proud mother,
an old keeper of death's wisdoms
alive still, and my eyes dazzle
because truth is not stones broken
or shrines razed, it is light blazing
through death, life, and the one vision
that keeps time with the stars dancing.

The Antispast is a foot of four syllables with the rhythm ˘ ´ ´ ˘.
The second line of the above is a quotation from Webster's *The Duchess of Malfi* and is catalectic, which is to say one syllable short.

Akroteri

Under the lava, the brown crust's carapace,
    Akroteri holds on.
Ripples of waves on the great jars' eloquence
    tell of men with strong hands
shaping the rhythms of earth-sea mastery,
    dolphins bearing stripped souls
over the oceans to bright light wakening
    life again to fresh dawns.
Sadly the frescoes are long gone — fisherman,
    boxer, dancer, wild bird,
elegant priestess, her poised hands offering
    incense, praising wise gods —
taken away to be stored, safe, gathering
    scholars' praise in dark rooms,
leaving the buckled and scarred walls' emptiness,
    broken lintels, wrenched stairs
here for our reverence. No grief troubles us.
    All that's gone is still here.
Earth has its memory. Light shines over us.
    Akroteri holds on.

There are several metres credited to Archilochus. This is one used by Horace. The first part of the line is dactylic tetrameter with a spondee for the third foot: ′ ◡ ◡ ′ ◡ ◡ ′ ′ ′ ◡ ◡ . The second part of the line is an Ithyphallic and is made up of either three trochees, or, most usually, two trochees and a spondee: ′ ◡ ′ ◡ ′ ′ .

Santorini

On the slopes are the vines
   circled around their mounds
as if baskets, the strands
   woven and plaited tight
for collecting the dew drops
   that the gods provide;
there's no river or good well
   and the rain's unknown.

Yet the grapes of these squat vines
   are as rich and strong
as those tangling the lush hills
   of the far away,
and from passion, from stooped skill,
   and from age on age
of their history wine flows
   in a golden tide.

The twelve syllable Asclepiadean Metre in Greek has the rhythm:
ᴗ ᴗ ◠ ᴗ ᴗ ◠ * ◠ ᴗ ᴗ ◠ ᴗ ◠. The Latin version of the metre substitutes
a spondee (◠ ◠) for the first foot and a spondee or a trochee (◠ ᴗ) for
the final one.

Poros, Recalling Demosthenes

I would speak to the pale ghost that was loosed
   here on the island height
if I thought he was still bound to his death-bed
   by desire or pride,
or perhaps by the sea god that possessed
   temple and spirit both,
for to die in a god's shrine is to place life
   in a grasping hand,
but to call to a dumb orator, (stone-dumb),
   is to question wind
as with mouthfuls of beach pebbles he made speeches
   against the sea
to be faced by a dead silence when sea's deity
   answered back
in a place that's become ruin, a bleak warning
   that speeches end.

The rhythm of this sixteen syllable Asclepiadean Metre runs: ⏑ ⏑ ´
⏑ ⏑ ´ ´ ⏑ ⏑ ´ ´ ⏑ ⏑ ´ ⏑ ´ .

After the Museum

A chill wine, a tall glass
   beneath tress, the time noon,

we sit silent, still dazed
   by old masks of torn gold,
by black vessels, taut figures
   of men, maidens, goats, gods,
our birth-world, our first thoughts.
   This fall morning has reached through
today's mind and pulled round
   our bent shoulders death's cloak
that thwarts time, allows hands
   to reach out and touch hands
and eyes, lips of past lives,
   our wives, husbands, priests, kings,
perhaps, even - here, there -
   our own selves, our eyes meeting
again over chill wine
   beneath trees as Pan's pipes
renew leaves or Zeus speaks
   in dark thunders. Stilled here,
we know earth, are earth's bones,
   beyond time, beyond truth.

The Bacchiac foot is also, confusingly, called an anti-bacchic and
has the rhythm ⏑ ⁄ ⁄. It is more common in Latin than in Greek
and is most usually found in tetrameters as here, (⏑ ⁄ ⁄ ⏑ ⁄ ⁄ ⏑ ⁄ ⁄
⏑ ⁄ ⁄).

BACCHICS
_____

Chant

Drink deep the dark vintage,
full crimson, blood-heavy;

sense earthen pulse rhythms,
hear songs of far caverns,
drum-thunders, clashed cymbals,
shrill pipes, and face knowledge
long-hidden, earth wisdoms.
Praise, praise the Great Goddess.

The Bacchic is a trisyllabic foot with the rhythm ✓ ✓ ◡ . The above
is Bacchic dimeter.

CHOLIAMBICS
_____

Island Harbour

I stare across the harbour
   thinking tides only
persist because the moon
   has laws beyond reason,
and reason hides away
   from dreams and blood's pulsebeat,
denying music's truth,
   but tides are time's music,
with drums and strings and wind
   exciting wild breakers,
or gently sighing, calm
   as flutes on far mountains
and trembling small waves rippling
   sandy shored islands,
they praise Selene riding
   over dark waters,
bare-faced or cloaked in darkness,
   crystal-browed goddess

of all our poems and songs;
   above the night harbour
she watches, changing shapes,
   transforming, creating.

The Choliambic (or Scazon) metre was adapted from the Greek by Catullus and Martial. The rhythm of each twelve syllable line is: ‿ ⁄ ‿ ⁄ ‿ ⁄ ‿ ⁄ ‿ ⁄ ⁄ ‿. The first, third, and final feet may be spondees (⁄ ⁄).

CHORIAMBIC DIMETER
_____

The Acropolis

Climbing the steps
   carved in the hill
golden with dust,
   history's dead;
seasonal change
   only implies
deaths and returns,
   cyclical shifts;
centuries, years,
   tell us no more.

Nevertheless,
   reaching the height,
looking across
   roofs to the sea,
origins fuse
   spirit and sense,
tremble the limbs,

> catch at the breath;
> nothing is lost;
> nothing is new.

The Choriamb is a metrical foot running ´ ˘ ˘ ´. Choriambic dimeter can be found in both Sappho and Horace, but also in some later accentual European verse, most notably in Goethe's *Pandora*. The caesura, as presented above by indenting half lines, is not essential.

CRETIC METRE

Alternatives

> Over there forest green
>   hides a well deep as night;
> tangled thick undergrowth
>   walls it round, keeps it whole.
>
> Over here shines a spring
>   pebbled, clear, known to all.
> Never touch, never drink;
>   search the wood, seek the well.

The Cretic metre is in lines of twelve syllables which may or may not have a caesura as here. The rhythm is: ´ ˘ ´ ´ ˘ ´ ´ ˘ ´ ´ ˘ ´.

Morning Song

Rapt in a dawn of beginnings
   I stand at the window renewing
time as I do every morning,
   reshaping the possible future.

Over the city the mountains
   are holy with snow in a radiance
brighter than dreams of the mystics
   entranced in their caverns of music.

Closer and smaller the snowdrops
   are bending in reverent wonder
over the earth that is stirring
   in labour, preparing its vision.

I at the window have little
   to give but the words of my waking
thankful for life that renews me
   to face an improbable future.

Dactylic Hexameter, the oldest known Greek metre, consists of six
dactyls with a caesura most usually in the third foot. The last and
sixth foot was often cut short by one syllable or made a spondee
(´´). The rhythm thus runs: ´◡◡ ´◡◡ ´◡ * ◡ ´◡◡ ´◡◡ ´◡
(or ´´).

Harbourside

Sipping dark red wine
  in the evening's cool calm,
dreaming youth's lost dreams
  as the harbour repeats waves,
ripples, slow, soft, slapping
  the base of the scarred wall,
time becomes blurred; voices
  are drifting and thin songs
hesitate, swerve, tremble
  along the steep streets
rising behind small bars
  and I touch with my old hand
polished, bright, smooth, silver,
  her emblem, an owl ring,
knowing all night's creatures
  in dream or awake still
kneel as moonrise alters
  the memory's slow tread,
shaping dark-eyed dancers
  alive to their past loves,
vanished pains, shames, laughters
  bringing a truth home:
All is flux, tide, change
  and today is a day past,
age a sea-swept mirror
  and dying a new song.

The rhythm of the Dactylo Epitrite is as follows: /˘// /˘˘ /˘˘ //, the first foot being an epitrite, the two following feet dactyls and the last foot a spondee. This metre is most frequently found in Pindaric odes. Occasionally, the last stressed syllable is omitted.

November

Again winter comes
   and rain smears the pane
as firs darken green
   and oaks bare their boughs.

The grey sea begins
   to gnaw crumbling cliffs,
to heave rocks and scoop
   out pools, gullies, caves,

while chill nights create
   a new store of dreams
for springtime to claim
   as truths born of love.

The Dochmius is a six syllable metrical foot with the rhythm ˘ ´ ´ ˘ ´. It can, therefore, be regarded as an anti-bacchic (˘ ´ ´) followed by an iamb (˘ ´).

Handfast

Give me your hand in this temple
   above the incurious ocean
here as the autumn retains
   wisdom in pillars of stone

mutely perhaps, but the silence
   is poised as if pause or hiatus
splitting a moment of time
   gathered from history's hoard.

Stand with me here and remember
   the morning you woke in a brightness,
feeling that nothing was there,
   vacuum, emptiness, space.

Timelessness works in this fashion,
   a fathomless well in the future,
present and past, and a word
   missing from all that's been said.

Give me your hand. It is wisdom
   that tells us our days and our years
end and begin in a place
   marrying never with now.

Love is both endless and timeless;
   we touch it together, renewing
faith in the power of life,
   trust in the silence of stones.

The Elegiac Couplet consists of two lines of verse, one a dactylic
hexameter and one a dactylic pentameter. The dactylic hexameter
runs: ´◡◡ ´◡◡ ´◡ * ◡ ´◡◡ ´◡◡ ´◡ (or ´´). The dactylic
pentameter runs: ´◡◡ ´◡◡ ´ * ´◡◡ ´◡◡ ´ (or ◡). A spondee
(´´) may be substituted for either the first or second foot, and the
last syllable may be a short one (i.e. unstressed).

Red Tree

On the slope of the hill as the sun sets
the bark of the tree has a red glow
and, becoming a pillar of fire, makes
in the stillness a temple, a place wise
as history's oracle, holds out
for a vanishing moment a god's hands
to bless us with strength from the earth's heart.

The Enoplius metre has the rhythm ⏑⏑′ ⏑⏑′ ⏑⏑′ ′, though the first foot may be replaced by an iamb (⏑′).

EPITRITE DIMETER I

Drowned Island

A tide slides over long drowned land,
the white stone houses turned weed-green,
the hacked walls crumbled, vines all gone,
an old old tale: the sun-blessed world
erupts, burns, drowns in sky-high seas,
becomes myth, spells the way time ends.

There are four epitrite feet. This is the first one and has the rhythm ⏑ ′ ′ ′.

Storm

Over still seas gather dark clouds;
winds have dropped; air's heavy, skin damp.
Clothing clings, chests heave to ease breath.
Far away, sheet lightning warns. Soon
single raindrops fall and time brings
roads awash, thin rivers swollen, trees downed,
freedom's long known need to break bonds.

This is the second Epitrite metre and has the rhythm ⏑̄ ⏑ ⏑̄ ⏑̄. In the sixth line a trochee (⏑̄ ⏑) has been inserted between the first and second foot of the dimeter.

Inconclusive

Walk slowly down Time's mountain track.
Death's ocean waits. Dark fathoms hold
bright wisdoms; no soul ever dies;
breath having gone, new breath begins.

The third Epitrite has the rhythm ⏑̄ ⏑̄ ⏑ ⏑̄.

November Once More

Leaves fall slowly, turn, twist, settle;
bared boughs glisten; rain, down-sliding
tiled roofs, shimmers; winds gust, threaten;
soon earth sleeps in deep midwinter.

The fourth Epitrite foot has the rhythm ╵ ╵ ╵ ⌣ .

Mykonos

By the still harbour of twilight
    I am half dazed by a name
that has called out from the dark alley
    behind whiteness of stone;
it's an old name with a far echo,
    not clear sound; it is more
of a wave breath or a carved shell
    than a known word I can say,
but it's Her name, and a true name,
    and I lift wine to the sky
here where curved boats in repose
    lie like wild things on the shore.

The Galliamb could also be described as ionic tetrameter catalectic, as it consists of four ionic feet, the last one being a syllable short: ⌣ ⌣ ╵ ╵ ⌣ ⌣ ╵ ╵ ⌣ ⌣ ╵ ╵ ⌣ ╵ ╵ . In this example, the third foot in the last line is an anti-bacchic (⌣ ╵ ╵).

At Rhodes

As I stand by the city wall
I envision a cell of peace
that's been hidden away for years;
it is hard to describe or name;
you could call it a sealed up shrine
of the light, a presence of stone
enclosing a secret place
where forbidden mysteries lie
and a memory sleeps and dreams.

In the lee of a twilit wall
that has time in its very touch
I am facing a stone retreat
and perceiving beneath its door
in a moment of truth a light
like the light on the swerving tide
where the harbour extends its arms
to horizons beyond our ken.

In the hush of remembered time
where the vivid colossus, god
of the sun in its glory, stood
I am staring on tide and moon
and futurity fills my mind
as it tells me beyond the door
at the last I will find my name
and unmask as I walk on the sea.

The Glyconic metre is composed in lines of eight syllables with
the rhythm ⌄⌄′ ⌄⌄′ ⌄′.

Girl Waiting

It is hard to believe the girl
that is leaning against the gold
sandstone pillar is truly young;
she has eyes of the old sea.

She is smiling a gentle smile;
an Etruscan has cast her face —
smooth bronze polished by years of need
and the touch of desire's hand.

There is nothing to hold me back
from becoming her latest love
but the knowledge that she is death
and her mind is a lost song.

If I went to her, told my name,
it would say to her spume and sand,
shoreline words that the tides erase,
and her kiss is a false coin.

But a lie can renew a truth;
as she turns her enquiring eyes,
wide, blue, mortal to touch my face,
I am tranced, for Artemis holds

in her quiver an arrow poised
for destruction of false desire,
and I watch as she moves away
down steep steps to the sea.

The Glyconic Stanza as invented by Anacreon, consists of three glyconics followed by a pherecratean. The Glyconic runs: ˘ ˘ ´ ˘ ˘ ´ ˘ ´. The first foot may be a molossus (´ ´ ´) and the last one a pyrrhic (˘ ˘). The pherecratean runs: ˘ ˘ ´ ´ ˘ ˘ ´ ´ ; a molossus may be substituted for the first foot and a trochee (´ ˘) for the last.

S w a l l o w s

Under the eaves of the house
swallows are building a nest,
molding a chamber of mud,
fragments of twigs and of straw
forming a pendulous ball,
droppings inscribing the sill
spelling a language of air
telling the wisdoms of wings.

Swallows are sacred in all
countries that know them of old,
priests of the house and the air,
guardians of hearth and of roof.

The Hemiepes metrical line is a dactylic trimeter catalectic, which is to say one with the concluding two unstressed syllables missing. The metre is ´ ˘ ˘ ´ ˘ ˘ ´ .

Nightwords

Light the lamp in the window; night will come soon;
dreams are crowding the shadow, tempting sleepers;
soft-mouthed, whispering, hinting names and features,
serpent, lover or stranger poise to alter
vision, shifting their shapes and melding together,
fusing present and past, the moment endless.

Night's deep messages challenge shallow daylight,
call dawn foolish, an empty superficial
way of looking, a kind of passing falsehood
they must counter to clear away confusion,
bring back goddess and god, the earth's perspectives,
teach proportion, design, the ancient stories
we repeat in our births, our deaths, our lifetimes.

The Hendecasyllabic line contains eleven syllables. The rhythmic pattern is most usually: ´˘ ˘˘ ´˘´ ˘´˘. There are many possible variations; the first foot may be a spondee (´´), a trochee (´˘), an iamb (˘´) or a pyrrhic (˘˘). The final syllable may be stressed or unstressed. Martial always began the line with a spondee and ended it with a stressed syllable.

IAMBELEGUS

The Deities

As men and words bowed low before
  wanderers bringing them sung

accounts of long gone times, the tunes
    faltering-bright in the throat,
so we, in Truth's high place are held
    rapt and entranced as the light
reveals the worn stone heads of gods
    poised on their pediments, calm,
to stare across more space than sky
    ocean or earth can provide,
and, gentle, lips curved firm with love,
    goddesses smiling, remote
as time, yet near, close, touching hearts,
    holding our dream in their hands.

The Iambeligus metre runs: ∪ ⁄ ∪ ⁄ ⁄ ⁄ ∪ ⁄ * ⁄ ∪ ∪ ⁄ ∪ ∪ ⁄ . It is
found in both Greek and Latin verse, and most notably in Horace.

IAMBIC TRIMETER

Aegina

When Britomartis
    fled the shore for wooded heights
and vanished wholly,
    island folk renamed her, said
Aphaia, goddess!
    Truth had come, unseen and pure.

They found the goddess
    hid from light, was never loud
outright or headstrong;
    shadow-cloaked and quick to hide,
half-heard she whispered,

murmured counsel, granted love.

The rustling branches,
  shaking grass, and drifting dust
above the harbour
  name, as twilight fades the red
sunset and brings night,
  all the ghosts unseen and true.

In Greek Iambic Trimeter, each rhythmic unit consists of two feet (a dipody) and not one, as in English prosody. There is a caesura after the fifth syllable. The rhythmic pattern, therefore, is: ˘´˘´ ˘ * ´˘´ ˘´˘´. The first foot may sometimes be ˘˘´˘´. There may be other feet substituted for the first half of the dipodies. The Latin version of this metre is termed a Senarius. This, however, is arranged as six separate feet (not dipodies) and spondees (´´) could replace iambs in the second and fourth feet.

Ionic a Majore

Chthonic

Creeds trouble the earth's harmony,
make rubble of rock certainties,
build shrines to possessed wanderers,
carve symbols on hacked masonry,
make even the roses blossoming
sharp-thorned in the hedge meaningful,
charge water with spells, magical
chants, rites, and proclaim holiness.

Earth, patient, retains tranquilness;

words, names are absurd entities —
far better accept quietude,
touch, handle the good energy,
say nothing but know mastery,
bless Time for its wise offering.

The Ionic A Majore foot is of four syllables with the rhythm ´ ´ ˘ ˘.
The above is a dimeter.

I O N I C   A   M I N O R E

N o c t u r n e

On the tall walls of the old town,
as the sun sets and the dusk slides
to the still streets, the untamed blooms
are a dance rippling as faint foam
on the shore's edge where the stones shine
in the last light and a man walks
with a slow dog and a bowed head.

The metrical foot, Ionic A Minore, has the structure ˘ ˘ ´ ´ . There
are two feet in each of the above lines.

In Homage

Dusk, ascending mountains,
western skies extending
shadow, sun declining,
speaks of Dionysus,
whispers vines are twining
round the dreams of lovers,
round the twilit houses,
blessing hill and harbour,
murmurs wanton pleasure
sanctifies the beaches,
makes the shingle glisten,
gives the ripples music,
knows the holy temple
holding wisdom's altar
needs no stony summit,
lives in human heartbeats
drumming celebration,
wears the wreath of glory
crowning Dionysus.

The Ithyphallic metre supposedly gets its name from being used in processions at the festival of Dionysus, at which the phallus was carried. It is commonly found in combination with other metres. The rhythm, using - to indicate an ancept or syllable which can be either stressed or unstressed, is: ´ ◡ ´ ◡ ´ -.

Contemplating It

Thinking of inadequately
passionate espousals and their
cumulating consequences
even the embarrassments of
bachelordom captivate him.

There are four Paeons. The one exemplified above is usually considered the first. It has the rhythm ´ ˘ ˘ ˘.

Rarely used as a metre in Greek, even in a simple dimeter as
here, it is extremely difficult to handle in English. Any sequence of
three unstressed syllables one is certain to be partially stressed. The
third syllable of the third line in this example is one of these.

Frivolity in Age

While thinking of my happiness
and wandering through memory
contentedly, I'm fashioning
a versicle in wonderment
that age can be so frivolous
when dying is a possible
conclusion to the quotable
and timelessness is happening.

This Paeon has the rhythm ˘ ´ ˘ ˘ and the lines are dimeters.

Island Temple

On the summit of the island
is the ruin of a temple
and a sacredness surrounds it,
an invisible dimension
of the Goddess in her glory
and the power of the island.

The rhythm of this Paeon is ˘ ˘ ˊ ˘ and the lines are dimeters.

Daybreak

At the conclusion of the dark
our irrepressible delight
in the emergence of the sun
is a defiance and a wish.

This Paeon has the rhythm ˘ ˘ ˘ ˊ and is here part of a dimeter.

Inscription

In the deep of the night or at high noon
the arrival of love is a death blow.

The Paroemiac (or anapaestic dimeter catalectic) consists of two,
two foot units, or dipodies, the second one being cut short, as in:
˘ ˘ ʹ ˘ ˘ ʹ ˘ ˘ ʹ   ˘ . The first anapaest (˘ ˘ ʹ) may be changed
into a spondee (ʹ ʹ) and the last syllable of all may be stressed. In
Greek literature, the paroemiac is often used for proverbs, as here.

Sky God

The sky above is
reflecting nothing,
itself reflected
in sea and river,
does not consider
our human follies
deserve attention;
remote and godlike
it shifts and changes
in wilful fashion —
— we think it wilful —
destroying, blessing
at whim; although we
attempt to guide it

with sacrifices
and feasts and dances
it won't consider
our human follies
deserve attention.

The Penthemimer Rhythm is as follows, using - to indicate an ancept, a syllable which may be either stressed or unstressed: - ´ ˘ ´ -. The Penthemimer is most usually presented with other metres and forms part, not the whole, of a line.

PHALAECEAN METRE

Lesbos

At my table beside the water mumbling
its soft syllables under stars pretending
to be distantly watching nothing mortal,
I remember a music-haunted island
and am pondering verses Sappho gave us,
not because of the wine or sliding waters
but this evening, having noticed lovers,
feeling grieved by the ache of other heartbreaks
and the clinical air of stars that watched her.

The Phalaecean metre is composed in 11 syllable lines the first two syllables and the last one being either stressed or unstressed, and here given the mark - . The metre runs: - - ´ ˘ ˘ ´ ˘ ´ ˘ ´ -.

In Darkness

Old wood creaks in the dark house,
tells night-thoughts to recall all
time's paths lead to the one place,
deep pools shining for ever.

The Pheracratean Metre is one of six syllables with the rhythm ´´
´ ˘ ˘ ´´, which is to say two spondees bracketing a dactyl (´ ˘ ˘).
The final spondee may be changed to a trochee (´ ˘), as in my
example. A pyrrhic (˘ ˘) may sometimes be substituted for the
first foot.

Expiation

In the deep of the night the wind
is a lash on the roof slates,

yet I know that the dawn will bring
us to peace when the dark's done,

for the guilts of the night prepare
us for innocence once more.

In the tree by the garden gate
there's a bird with an old tune.

This metre consists of a glyconic followed by a pherecratean. The rhythm of the glyconic is: ˘ ˘ ´ ˘ ˘ ´ ˘ ´. A molossus (´ ´ ´) may be substituted for the anapaest of the first foot and a pyrrhic (˘ ˘) for the trochee of the last one. The pheracratean rhythm is: ˘ ˘ ´ ˘ ˘ ´ ´ ; a molossus may be substituted for the first foot and a trochee (´ ˘) for the last.

Prosodion

Apollo, Apollo, return
your music to words that they sing
with clarity, sweetness and strength,
transforming the mind and the heart,
releasing the day from its worn
old fetters of usury, cant,
political greed and despair.
Apollo, Apollo, reshape
our minds that they understand earth,
air, water and fire, and revere
the spirit of life and the need
of Time to be healed by delight.
Apollo, Apollo, be near
as children forget how to dance
and song is destroyed on the winds
that blow from the end of the world.

The Prosodion is a song performed by a chorus before an altar or moving towards it, and it was devoted to the worship of Apollo. The rhythm is ˘ ´ ˘ ˘ ´ ˘ ˘ ´ , though the initial iamb may sometimes be replaced by a spondee, and this metre is prosodiakon or prosodiacus.

Aegean Interlude

The small harbour is pale stone,
its hewn masonry timeless,
and tides moving beneath walls
surge, swell, slither and ripple
to sway murmurous old songs,
our lives restless, uneasy
as boats rising and falling.

The Reizianum metre is a Telesillian metre with the final syllable omitted. The rhythm runs ˘ ´ ´ ˘ ˘ ´ ´, but the first foot may be a spondee (´ ´) or a pyrrhic (˘ ˘) and the last foot may be a trochee (´ ˘). I have used these variations in the above example. This metre was used by Plautus in combination with iambic and anapestic metres.

RHOPALIC VERSE

Academic Note

This canting professor, supposedly intellectual,
a scholar, considers phonology ineffectual.

A line of Rhopalic Verse is made up of words which proceed from monosyllable, to disyllable, to trisyllable and so on. It rarely appears more than once in any passage of verse. It can be found in both Homer and Virgil.

The Isles of Greece

For Yannis Goumas

Temples lifting pillars above the dark sea,
ruins torn by weathers of tireless ages,
shine in silence, keeping their seamless wisdom
safe from our blunders.

Stone itself is equally non-committal,
crumbling slowly under the wind's caresses,
scouting all of history's bland pretensions,
mythical glories.

Spiders' long legs, motionless lines of shadow,
hint at nothing, carefully poised and waiting,
nets prepared with elegance, tautly silver,
death an amusement.

Only slow dust drifting around our footsteps,
little lizards scurrying under marble,
have an air of offering teasing answers,
sly and evasive.

Gods are fond of mockery; many stories
tell of laughter, ridicule. Here, however,
smiles are gentle; dust is the final fable;
nothing's eternal,

nothing, nothing, nothing....We hear the echo
sounding down the centuries, Lear once more
mad as mad, but bringing to all the questions

splendours beyond them.

Here in old stone temples above the harbours
patient gods and goddesses keep that secret;
life transforming life is the only wisdom,
making it holy.

Sapphics are composed in four line stanzas, the rhythm of the first three lines being ´˘ ´˘ ´˘˘ ´˘ ´˘ , though ´´ may be substituted for the second and fifth feet. The fourth line consists of a dactyl followed by a trochee, ´˘˘ ´˘ , though the final foot may sometimes be a spondee, ´´ .

SATURNIAN METRE

The Statue

Alone within a moment
   filched from time and duty,
I pause beside Apollo's
   garden statue standing
where hedge and oak and chestnut
   tangle greens to shade him
from hungry sunlight searing
   sacred flanks of marble,
and feel myself becoming
   old as him or older,
the moss that stains his sandals,
   smears of spreading lichen,
and bruises, little fissures,
   scars of mine though hidden
from people's eyes, forgotten

largely till Apollo
decides to tease, remind me
　gods and poets can't alter
the ways of time; though artful
　tricks delay extinction
there's no escape from hurting,
　none from degradation,
and time will trash the garden,
　burn the books and statues.

The Saturnian Metre appears to be the earliest Latin metre known and the only one not based upon Greek structures. Its rhythmic pattern is generally agreed to be: ˘́ ˘́ ˘́˘ * ́˘́ ˘́˘ .

SENARIUS METRE

Hydra

Go down the great hill, find the boats that hymn the sea,
upcurving prows that answer moving winds and tides
with dip and sway, accepting gently dancing waves,
responding still to ancient rhythms, pipes and drums
recalled from fireside stories celebrating gods
whose vows protect the harbours, bringing oil and wine.

The Senarius Metre is one of twelve syllables with the rhythmic pattern -´ ˘́ -´ ˘́ -´ ˘́ , the - standing for a syllable which may be either short (unstressed) or long (stressed).

Skolion

At the close of the day in ease and gladness
I am lifting my glass to praise the great god
and the vine and good wine in the glass
shining and red and strong,
vivid and pure and red.

Now the night is our cloak, with cheerful laughter
I am breaching the bottle, praising good thirst,
and the talk and warm friendship and love
blessing the days to come
drinking the dark away.

The Skolion is a drinking song with a mixed metre. The first two lines are Phalaecean and scan as follows, using - to denote a syllable that may be stressed or unstressed: -- ´˘˘ ´˘ ´˘ ´-.
　　The following line has the rhythm ˘˘´ ˘´ ´˘˘´ and the stanza concludes with two lines, each with the rhythm ´˘˘ ´˘´.

What The Rain Says

Wet autumn asserts gravely
　　that melancholy brings wise
minds knowledge, the earth's future
　　perceived clearly in drowned leaves.

The Latin Sotadean metre is composed in fourteen syllable lines with the rhythm ´ ´ ˇ ´ ´ ˇ ´ ´ ˇ ´ ´ . The third foot may be changed into two trochees (´ ˇ ´ ˇ) as occurs in the work of Martial.

In this example the first line has this variation.

TELESILLIAN

Temple of the Goddess

The long climb up the mountain side
accepts sky as a way to sense
Her blue robe and Her blazing crown,
Her far sight with no limits known.

Arrived, pillars are broken, stained,
and courtyards are uneven, cracked;
no rain blesses the arid earth
and each word is a breath of dust.

The Great Goddess has gone away
we're told sadly, and nothing's left
of old truths but inscriptions scarred
on stone fragments, their meanings lost.

They lie. Under our feet, above
our heads viewing the topless columns,
on each side and before, behind,
the Great Mother is present, whole.

Her strength, vision, undying love
and clear mercy complete our lives
with death, destiny shaped and sure,

and each death with ensuing birth.

We stand blessed by a wisdom past
that today's wisdom must understand
if Earth Goddess and Goddess Earth
are to keep safe what is left to save.

The Telesillean metre is given its name because of a woman poet of
Argos, Telesilla, who lived in the fifth century, B.C. The metre is
actually a glyconic with the first unstressed syllable omitted, and
runs: ⌣ ′ ′ ⌣ ⌣ ′ ⌣ ′. The first foot may be a spondee (′ ′). In the
example here the last line departs from the rule by being an ortho-
dox glyconic.

TROCHAIC TETRAMETER

In The Museum

White cycladic figures honour
   shelves of glass, museum-trapped
anaconic faces shaping
   stillness progress threw away,
craving colour, noise, discarding
   simple gestures, gentle words.
Now, outside the huge museum,
   traffic rumbles, ashes fall,
posters shriek of death and passion,
   garish features glossed with paint,
yet the faceless shining figures
   poised behind the polished glass
radiate a stronger passion
   unified by time and space

praising earth and sky and ocean,
   folding flame in cradling arms,
nameless knowing every human
   name and need and sharing all.

The Greek Trochaic Tetrameter consists of four feet each of which contains two trochees, apart from the final foot which is cut short. Thus each foot is, in fact, two feet or a dipody. The metre runs: ´ ⌣ ´ ⌣   ´ ⌣ ´ ⌣   *   ´ ⌣ ´ ⌣   ´ ⌣ ´ . Anapaests (⌣ ⌣ ´) were sometimes substituted for the second, fourth, or fifth dipody. Tribrachs (⌣ ⌣ ⌣) were also substituted frequently.

VERSUS SPONDAICUS

Day's End

Red skies make trees stark black.
   Long grass turns grey, sighs, fades.
Night nears. Trees wear dark's cloak,
   lose form; wind stilled, leaves carve
spear shapes, haunt air. Moon light
   slides through curved boughs, pales grass,
hones leaves, slants shade down paths,
   stains lawns. Dream stirs, shape-shifts;
hands reach, eyes gaze, masks swim
   night's tides, spell truth, spill lies.

According to one authority, this Latin verse form is composed of six spondees: ´ ´   ´ ´   ´ ´   *   ´ ´   ´ ´   ´ ´ , as here. Another view is that the term Versus Spondaicus describes a dactylic hexameter with a spondee instead of a dactyl as its fifth foot.

CORNISH

No End To It

Some things remain
as aftermath, an unwanted stain
on pillow or sheet
making it clear
that for us, here,
no ending is ever complete.

Always there are
the continuing, if minor, scar,
the snagged thread,
the aftertaste;
even dreams linger, must be outfaced
before leaving bed.

Each time we make an end
we try to pretend
there are actual conclusions,
even while knowing
wherever we are going
yesterdays intrude their delusions.

This Cornish verse form was current in the fourteenth century. The lines may be of any length from four to nine syllables, and the rhyme scheme is A A B C C B.

C Z E C H

Fourteenth Century Traditional Couplets

Bonfire Day

Held, as Autumn leaves were turning
bronze and gold, by thoughts of burning
pyres' heroic executions,
villains victims of dark passions,
human torches, crisp October
prelude, overture, disturber,
boys, for weeks forgetting childhood,
changed, became a begging priesthood
crying out for pennies, shillings,
rags and tatters, cast-off clothing,
planning ritual destructions,
eyes alight with conflagrations
wild November brought, renewing
ancient rites for boyhood's doing.

This verse form is composed of octosyllabic rhyming couplets in trochaic tetrameter (´˘ ´˘ ´˘ ´˘).

ENGLISH

A Birthday Card

Jar after jar in the Magic Sticks
Observed us making, mending verses,
Honoring Liam's Dolmen Press,
Needling Dublin with afflatus.

Muse-haunted, too, in other worlds—
Ontario, British Columbia, France—
Nurtured upon Her sorceries
Together we trod out the dance,
Avid to achieve success,
Greedy for all words could disclose;
Undone by distance, John, I bless
Each memory more than you suppose.

The usual Acrostic is a verse that spells out a name or a message with the first letters of each line. It is commonly used for tributes.

There are other more complicated acrostics, such as one in which both the opening and closing letters of the lines spell out a message and another in which this task is performed by letters in the middle of the lines. Yet others spell out a message by using the first letter of the first line, the second of the second line and so forth.

A footnote may be needed to the above verse. The Magic Sticks was a name given to the Majestic Hotel, now no longer standing.

Herself: A Footnote

This century or that, this place or another,
the story is the same: She as the great mother
of god or gods or earth, She as the bright maiden,
the bride, the beloved, as the wise old woman,
midwife and death-cleanser; these are our histories,
our poems, our symphonies, undying mysteries.

The Alexandrine is a twelve syllable line with a caesura after the sixth syllable. Though no metre is designated, in English the Alexandrine is usually iambic. This is not so in French.

BALLAD

A Ballad of Despair

Mercy, Pity, Peace, and Love.
   I met a walking man.
He walked each street towards despair
   and stared up at the sun.

This way he walked. A sawdust head
   knocked on his coughing chest.
A hand twitched like an empty glove.
   A boot scratched at the dust.

That way he was. He was that way.
   Flame throbbed within his head.

The wax mouths of his five children
  spoke like they were dead.

'The Lamb that died' the preacher said.
  He saw the Lamb that died.
There was a black cloud round its head,
  a law book at its side.

'Love your neighbour', said the preacher,
  'and obey the Law.'
He saw the blinded fishermen
  die on the green shore.

He saw his brother spitting sand
  with barbed wire round his head.
His hands like rags turned his door key.
  His mouth shone like lead.

He climbed the stair. At the first step
  He saw a city burn.
Children with flesh like trailing rags
  watched him from the turn.

The second step he took, the sea
  delivered up its dead.
the shoals of miles shone their white bellies
  at the staring head.

And the third step he climbed, he stopped.
  He stood stiff as a door.
A thousand blinded tongueless creatures
  coupled on the floor.

He stopped, then climbed. He went into
  the room his children lay.
He knew that he was mad as truth

to take their lives away.

He knew that truth was mad. He walked
    the darkness of the street,
cried, 'Suffer the little children
    to die in a clean sheet.'

He climbed the headline steps outside
    the black industrial hall,
cried, 'Though the children ask for bread,
    what bread is there not stone?'

What bread not stone? I met him dressed
    in pity and in blood.
I met him knelt in Calvary Place
    beside his children's bed.

Mercy, Pity, Peace, and Love,
    I saw him lift his gun.
He lay like logic in the street
    and stared at the blind sun.

The Ballad is usually in quatrains, the first and third lines having
eight syllables and the second and fourth lines six. This is handled
very loosely; there are many variations. The most common rhythm
is iambic tetrameter alternating with iambic trimeter, thus: ⌣ ⁄ ⌣ ⁄
⌣ ⁄ ⌣ ⁄ ⌣ ⁄ ⌣ ⁄ ⌣ ⁄.

    This is handled freely. Some stanzas may be trochaic or be
dominated by dactyls or spondees.

    The rhyme scheme of the quatrains is A B C B.

The Farewell

I talk of *Amours de Voyage*. You shake your head,
admitting ignorance. I feel the bruise
spread through the fingers that accept the book.
Your body, stiffened by those Northern snows,
cannot believe in Mediterranean ease
and antiquarian elegance. Your eyes
expect the green of ice, the iron trees
black-spurred against the roar of cutting wind.
Voices come down from there. The joy of dogs.
The broken windows. All the rubbled creeds
in hugger-mugger, whiskey-drunk. You shake
your head again, hair like a copper wave
burnished and burning. There is little use
in talk of elegance, of poised control,
where icepacks loom. You cannot find a track
that does not lead you through the blinded snows
to solitude, the blow upon the face,
the rending animals, the boot and claw.
You smile as children smile when tears are done,
less to reward than comfort those who must
not learn the heart's a stone. Your hand is cold.
No one can ever dispossess their world
for any other. Neither Clough nor I.
My farewell spreads its stain across your sky
but does not change it. Conversation veers.
We'll meet again perhaps. A couple of years.
Three at the most. When I return. Who knows?
I watch you walk away into the snows.

Blank Verse is unrhymed iambic pentameter (˘ ′ ˘ ′ ˘ ′ ˘ ′

⌣ ◌) and is characterized by a good deal of variation. It might better be described as ten syllable lines with iambic dominance.

Autumn Rain

For Anne Kelly

Fat raindrops slither down the pane;
sly raindrops wriggle down the pane;
Autumn has brought gentleness again.

The summer sun that burned the grass is gone;
the sun that ate away the grass is gone;
the sky is veiled and dreamy with compassion

for soon these leaves will wither and will fall;
these leaves will surely wither up and fall
and Winter will bring darkness on them all.

The Blues Stanza follows the pattern established by singers of the blues. There are three lines in each stanza. The first two lines end with the same word and second line is either a total or partial repetition of the first. The third line which rhymes with the previous two forms a conclusion to its predecessors or a development of them. There is no rule as to number of syllables or metre.

In Twilight

The leaves of willow twist and quiver
to the Spring song of the river
and the aspiring reed-beds shiver
beyond measure
as the winds of twilight give a
sigh of pleasure

for they're free at last to wander,
shape themselves to shadows, ponder
whispers in the grasses, wonder
if the dreaming
darkness, nearing, tugs asunder
twilit seeming

as neither one thing nor the other,
neither day nor dark, soon over,
a passing phase of leaf or lover,
grave or garden,
though it's in twilight we discover
truths that pardon.

The Burns Stanza is so called because Robert Burns made brilliant use of it and it was through his work that it became familiar. It is also called Standard Habbie, the Scots stanza and the six-line stave. Each stanza has six lines rhyming A A A B A B. The A lines are usually of eight or nine syllables and the B lines of four or five. This stanza may also be found in Provencal verse of the 11th century.

Carol for Yule

The bonfires of midwinter burn;
we conjure up the sun's return.

This is the black depth of the year
in which the seasons, circling near,
are pulled into the vortex; here
the bonfires of midwinter burn.

The quickening spirits of the Spring
whirl round their bright bewildering,
and with the energies they bring
we conjure up the sun's return.

The summer's heavy heat and bloom
is swept into December's gloom
and heady ripeness fills the room.
The bonfires of midwinter burn.

The fallen leaves and fruits of Fall
attend us, and, as we recall
that grey rain's every drifting shawl,
we conjure up the sun's return.

We gather round the towering tree
in whose perpetual green we see
this old earth's ancient potency.
The bonfires of midwinter burn.

The radiant necklace threaded bright
within the leaves reclaims delight

for darkness and within its light
we conjure up the sun's return.

Traditions ancient as the earth
tell how within this cold and dearth
there is miraculous rebirth.
The bonfires of midwinter burn,

and we lift up our voices to
the heart of life that will renew
itself in us and all we do.
The bonfires of midwinter burn;
we conjure up the sun's return.

While Carol is now a general term for a song at (usually) Christmas, the term was once more precise and described a poem beginning with a *texte* of two rhyming lines (A A) and continuing with quatrains rhyming B B B A, C C C A, the A lines being repetitions of one of the two lines of the texte, usually alternating as the poem proceeds. The complete texte may be repeated from time to time, as may other lines.

CAROL II _____

In The Hospice

Is it here that I will find
all dispute and all doubt refined
into pure clarity of mind?
  Is it here?

The twilit room is cool and still

and time seems ready to fulfil
the long-held hopes of heart and will.
   Is it here?

Outside my window shadow drifts
between the trees and Venus lifts
above the roofs as balance shifts.
   Is it here?

Years have scurried past like days
with failures, fantasies, delays,
and I have asked a hundred ways,
   Is it here?

It must be close. The mirror's shine
is trembling as if by design,
yet that face surely is not mine?
   Is it here?

Is it here and come at last?
The present moment trembles, vast
with all the future, all the past.
   Is it here?

The universe has shed its mask.
I step towards a different task,
yet one in which I still must ask,
   Is it here?

Another Carol form consists of quatrains rhyming A A A B, the B
line being a short line and an exact repetition of the beginning of
the first A line. This form may have been invented by Wyatt who
makes use of it.

Sun Setting

For Sylvia

Gradually the daylight leaves
the house behind us as we stroll
the garden, love confirmed and whole;
gradually the daylight leaves

the house behind us as we stroll,
our love grown stronger with the years
of pain and pleasure; darkness nears
the house behind us as we stroll,

our love grown stronger with the years;
gradually the daylight leaves
us with a wisdom that believes
our love grown stronger with the years.

Gradually the daylight leaves
the house behind us as we stroll
the garden, love confirmed and whole;
gradually the daylight leaves.

The Catena Rondo is my own invention. The metre is not prescribed, but the poem is in quatrains rhyming A B B A. The first line
of each quatrain is also the last one, and the second line of each
quatrain forms the first (and therefore also the fourth) of the next.
The final stanza should be an exact repetition of the first. The name
of the form is a combination of Catena (chain) and Rondo (circle)
because the stanzas are linked together by repetition and the poem
makes a circle by returning to its beginnings.

The Daybreak

For Michael Seward Snow

Before
the yellow dawn
reshapes the trees and roofs,
content to stain the edge of air,
I lie

exposed
to final dream,
aware of coming light,
and plan a slow exchange of time
with dawn.

A Cinquain is a poem or stanza of five lines with the syllable count 2 4 6 8 2. Originally used loosely to refer to any five line poem or stanza, this form was regularized by Adelaide Crapsey, who established it as having the syllable count given above, and as being unrhymed and in iambic metre.

Other users of the form have used looser metres and some cinquains have been rhymed.

At Dawn

Each dawn
I turn to the sun
in awe, and, not yet done
with dreaming, my dazed mind moves on
through dawn

to far
worlds beyond this
small troubled universe,
places of truth and timelessness
poised far

from here
time-whipped, clock-tamed,
confused, afraid, ashamed,
places that heal what we have maimed
down here

though dreams
move us to find
ways to change humankind,
shape faiths that will not mar or bind
our dreams.

The Cinquain may be rhymed in several ways. The A B B B A pattern is not uncommon.

Penny Whistle

A penny whistle in the dusk
below my window sill,
a simple tune that stops and starts
with no particular skill,

and yet each broken air and phrase
clearer than any bird
full-throated in the morning hush,
surpasses thought and word,

hints dancing bracken in the hills
and hidden streams that slake
the wanderer with stretched cupped hands
who has a heart to break

as do I, leaning on the sill,
no longer old and grey
but setting out upon the path
to meet what comes my way.

Common measure is composed in quatrains rhyming A B C B, the
first and third lines being iambic tetrameters (˘ ´ ˘ ´ ˘ ´ ˘ ´) and
the second and fourth lines iambic trimeters (˘ ´ ˘ ´ ˘ ´).

In Summary

1

Edgar Allen Poe
saw that all men here below,
the victims of shames and desires,
light their own pyres.

2

Saint Joan
accepted the flames, alone
with the absolute certainty
of Deity.

3

Thomas Lovell Beddoes
used to caper in the meadows
whenever he had satisfied his urge
to compose a dirge.

4

Paul Cezanne
is the painter than
whom no one gets greater
by happening later.

The Clerihew, most probably invented by Edmund Clerihew
Bentley, consists of two rhyming couplets, the first line being a

person's name, and the remaining three being biographical or anecdotal. It is almost invariably a frivolous form, but can be used seriously. The rhyming lines should be of different lengths.

CUMULATING VERSE

Again October

October winds transform the air,
bare swaying branches as they tear
leaves into flight; once more I stare,

triumphant, joyful, for I own
these colours — gold, bronze, every tone —
and every trodden husk and stone

as birthright; born this month, I owe
these winged leaves everything I know
and poems have brought me, yet the snow

must bring my anthems to their end
and gales no longer rage and rend
when silence meets me like a friend.

There are no rules as to syllable count and metre in Cumulating verse. The only rule concerns rhyme. In each stanza the rhyming end words are lengthened by an additional initial consonant as the verse proceeds.

Cumulating rhyme is the exact opposite or complement of Diminishing verse.

Churchgoing

For John Betjeman

Bent above pew and choir stall
he speaks as if his Christ were tall
beside him, caring for us all,

and though the sermon's old and stale
we cannot quite dismiss his tale,
but later, over snuggery ale,

protected from the night air's chill,
we think about that lonely hill
and pray good yet may come of ill.

In Diminishing verse, there are no rules as to syllable count or
metre. The only rule concerns rhyme. In each stanza the succeeding rhyme words are shortened, the initial sounds being removed
one by one.

Diminishing verse is commonly presented in rhyming triplets.
The best known example in English is George Herbert's *Paradise*.

True Story

He, though impoverished, had a title, and
she, though a commoner, owned vast tracts of land;

they answered all enquiries with a bland
well-phrased affection and contrived to blend
their differences so smoothly as to lend
their mutual hatred courtesy till the end.

DISYLLABICS

The Roses

For Anne Kelly

Roses
always
leave us;

sun-smoothed
petals
tumble

down through
changing
branches,

give earth
bitter
blessings.

Do not
send her
roses.

Disyllabics are lines of verse containing only two syllables. The second and fourth stanzas (and possibly the fifth) begin with spondees (´ ´); the remainder are trochees (´ ˘). This could, therefore, be described as trochaic monometer, with some substitution.

Two Poets of Canada

1

Canada, Canada,
Dorothy Livesay
titled her volume *The
Unquiet Bed*,

much of it splendidly
hypertempestuous,
some of it bringing the
blood to the head.

2

Canada, Canada,
Margaret Avison,
carefully culling each
brilliant line,

being excessively
hypermeticulous,
rarely presents us with
gems from her mine.

The Double Dactyl was invented by Anthony Hecht and John

Hollander and first disseminated in their anthology *Jiggery Pokery* (1967). It begins with a nonsense word which is a double dactyl. Common words are Jiggery Pokery and Higgledy Piggledy. I have chosen Canada Canada. The second word must consist of a persons name, which is also a double dactyl, as is the third line. The fourth line is a dactyl followed by a stressed syllable and is, therefore, a choriamb. The second quatrain follows the same pattern, but the second line must consist of one word. In some cases the first line is composed of one word. Only the fourth and eighth lines rhyme. The metre is therefore: ′ ⌣ ⌣ ′ ⌣ ⌣ * ′ ⌣ ⌣ ′ ⌣ ⌣ * ′ ⌣ ⌣ ′ ⌣ ⌣ * ′ ⌣ ⌣ ′ .

ECHO VERSE I

The Dark Well

Questioning is my task.
  Ask!
What should I seek in the heart?
  Art.
What are the heart's replies?
  Lies.
Is there a vision to know?
  No!
What do the stars portend?
  End.

The only structural rule of Echo verse is that the final syllable or syllables of the line must repeat exactly the immediately preceding sound. Echo verse frequently takes the form of a question and answer as in this example. George Herbert used this approach in *Heaven*.

Oracle

She is, as in fable, able
to play necromancer, answer
questions deep as gold, old
as time itself. She is earth, birth,
life, love without flaw, law.
What is the message of breath? Death.
And that of death? A flight, light.
Listen to her. Never ever
are her quiet replies lies.
Her shrine is the centre. Enter.

This is the second form of Echo verse, one in which the repeated sound is part of the continuing sentence structure and not a one word answer to a question.

The Rain

I hear the rain
drum, drum the roof over my head,
and think again
of that grey-lit day and the dead
man lapped in his casket of lead.

But feel no grief;
the downpour seemed measured to bless

and bring relief
with its deep cleansing timelessness
freeing the soul from all duress.

The drum of rain
on the lid of the coffin brought
his words again,
"Birth and death are a single thought."
A twig taps at the window pane.

English Quintet I is composed of five lines:
    Syllable count: 4 8 4 8 8
    End rhymes: A B A B B
    An English Quintet is any five line stanza with the above rhyme
scheme. The number of syllables may vary. The above example
follows the pattern set by Edmund Waller in the best known example of the form, *Go Lovely Rose*. There is no rule as to metre.

ENGLISH QUINTET II

In Plain Words

Let me say it clearly
(you may say it too)
I am almost nearly
half in love with you.
Of course, you knew.

It sounds a little stupid
(corny, you would say)
to blame it upon Cupid
or Destiny today,

but perhaps I may

since this is just a letter
(you may write one too)
suggesting that we'd better
do what lovers do,
and quickly too.

English Quintet II is composed of five lines:
   Syllable count: 6(2) 5 6(2) 5 4
   End rhymes: A   B   A   B B
   Here, only the first stanza keeps strictly to the syllable count,
but as the definition of an English Quintet is simply a five line
stanza with the rhyme scheme as given this is of no consequence.

HEROIC COUPLETS
_____

A b o v e

A man is walking up above my head
with a deliberate steady measured tread.

I put my part-read book down on my chair
and face the sunset window's dull red glare.

The steps grow louder, louder, and become
insistent as a dark and ritual drum.

Back and forth they travel, forth and back,
condemned to take some predetermined track.

I cannot read my book, nor can I stir;

step follows step and nails me to my chair.

The window darkens slowly into night.
I must break free of this, turn on the light.

I summon up my will and am released.
The light is on. The steady steps have ceased.

I breathe the silence — yet what is that sound?
Another step is pacing round and round.

I listen; it is quick and sharp and light.
A woman's heels are tapping out the night.

Where has she come from, and where has he gone?
The quick heels tap, tap, tap, tap on and on.

And now are joined by his more heavy tread,
crossing and circling there above my head,

monotonous, perpetual, on bare floor.
Dare I ascend the stair, knock on the door,

disrupt the measured drumming of their tread,
complain, appeal. The book I have not read

lies whitely open on the polished floor
where I am pacing, hearing more and more

insistently the quick steps and the slow
accompanying my own footsteps, and I know

they will not, cannot stop. No more can I.
A hunters moon is rising in the sky.

Heroic Couplets are rhyming couplets in iambic pentameter, and are usually made harmonious by various substitutions.

HUDIBRASTIC VERSE

The Welcome

With what a welcome should one greet a
difficult importunate metre
knocking at one's bolted door
asking two dozen lines or more
stating there is much of merit
to be gained by the proper spirit
with which one accepts instruction
without rebellion or ruction?
The appropriate mouthing should
be rhymed, of course, and if one could
insert a neat adverbial clause
to make Miltonic adepts pause,
or start each line with the same letter
like Dafyd ap Gwilym, so much the better.
The rule for ceremonial verse
is to be windy, never terse,
be complicated, clever, quick
to turn a trick of rhetoric,
be fulsome, flowery, fantastic
(don't worry if some flowers are plastic),
and if all inspiration's fled
borrow a bon mot from the dead —
what could be livelier and subtler,
for instance, than some Samuel Butler?

Hudibrastic verse is named after the satirical poem, *Hudibras*, by

Samuel Butler (1612-1680). It consists of rhyming octosyllabic couplets with a metre that swings easily from iambs to trochees and not infrequently includes variants. The form is essentially colloquial and it is impossible to see it as a vehicle for anything but jocularity and satire.

In Memoriam Stanza

Obiter Dicta

I cannot prove an honest thought
   and nor can any man alive;
   to think is always to contrive
and to contrive is to be bought.

We love each other — that is true;
   there's not a single speck of doubt,
   but when we ask what love's about
you trouble me, I trouble you.

There are no certainties to learn;
   however firmly we are taught
   that one away from one is nought,
the Krakatoan oceans burn.

The *In Memoriam* Stanza is so called after Tennyson's poem of that title. It is written in iambic tetrameter (˘ ´ ˘ ´ ˘ ´ ˘ ´) and in quatrains with the rhyme scheme A B B A.

Dramatis Personae

A breathless young lady named Ann
gasped out, when they asked why she ran,
"They say its a fact
that fast women attract
so I'm running as fast as I can."

A tiresome person called Claude
said "Frankly, I'm terribly bored;
there's nothing exciting
about all this fighting
and Superman's clearly a fraud."

The limerick form was popularized by Edward Lear in his *Book of Nonsense* (1846), but it can be found in print as early as 1821. Nowadays, it is used almost exclusively as a vehicle for bawdy verse, though there are some notable limericks by academic wits. The first two and the last lines of this five verse from have the metre: ˘ ˘ ´ ˘ ˘ ´ ˘ ˘ ´ though the unstressed syllables are often partly stressed and there is a good deal of substitution. The second and third lines have the metre ˘ ˘ ´ ˘ ˘ ´ ˘ most frequently. These metrical rules are not hard and fast; indeed, it could be said that metrically the limerick is based upon a repetition of anapaests (˘ ˘ ´) and little else. The rhyme scheme is strict, however: A A B B A. The limerick has been compared to the Madsong Stanza as a form.

In Those Days

With simple music, simple words
he tried to keep the dark at bay,
saw no need for complexities
when light had fallen from the day

and draughts were whispering at the ear
the riddling intricacies of death
and candles made the shadows move
around the room in every breath,

but Love, O Love and Spring, O Spring,
he sang around the cheating fire
and dressed the dreams of every soul
in simple fineries of desire.

Long Measure consists of quatrains of iambic tetrameter (˘ ´ ˘ ´ ˘ ´ ˘ ´) rhyming A B C B. Long Hymnal Measure differs from it only in having the rhyme scheme A B A B.

Narcissist

With a second line by Theodore Roethke

My self my own and only source of pride,

I spend myself in mirrors like a whore,
reflection laughing at the mounting score.

There is no mirror that I have denied
full payment of extravagances, for
I spend myself in mirrors like a whore,
reflection laughing at the mounting score.

I have ridden vanity like a tide
towards the ever heart-rewarding shore,
stood tall, and set out on the tide once more,
myself my own and only source of pride.
I spend myself in mirrors like a whore,
reflection laughing at the mounting score.

This example of the English Madrigal consists of thirteen lines of iambic pentametre (˘ ´ ˘ ´ ˘ ´ ˘ ´ ˘ ´) arranged in three sections of three, four, and six lines respectively. The rhyme scheme is as follows, the large capital letters representing repeated lines:

A B B2 * A B B B2 * A B B A B B2.

Though the term Madrigal was used somewhat loosely in the Elizabethan period, it has been asserted by Lewis Turco that the true Madrigal is in the form given here, and originated with Chaucer.

N O V E M

Time Passing

Leaves loll, weary;
a petal falls;
July is done.

I pick pebbles
from supple pools,
praising the tides.

We bless harvest
with simple tunes,
pacing the fields.

Last leaves scatter
crisp along lanes;
autumn tells lies.

Mists of morning
mount nameless hills,
claiming the dawn.

The cold creates
carved frozen forms,
captures our breath.

Wet snow slithers;
smooth branches shine;
slowly spring nears.

The Novem is my own invention, but derives from the Burmese Than-Bauk in its use of syllabic shapes (rather than rhyme). It consists of three unrhymed lines, each line containing three words. In the first line, the last word is the only one that is disyllabic. In the second line the second word has two syllables and in the third it is the first word that has this characteristic. Each stanza is bound together by consonance; a particular consonant is repeated four or five times.

Lest we Forget

Shame, remember
ember and flame;
flame and ember
remember shame!

A palindrome in poetry, is a verse that, when read either backwards or forwards, makes the same statement. The most well known palindrome in English is "Madam, I'm Adam". The above example is not a perfect palindrome as the first sentence, when reversed, produces a different message, though a complimentary one. Moreover, the reversal is in terms of complete words and not letter by letter.

SHORT MADRIGAL

Night Piece

I have been dreaming half the night
of holding you beside the sea
and watching waves crash into light.

I do not know how I can write
of that heart-pounding mystery;
I have been dreaming half the night
of holding you beside the sea

and wondering if those breakers might

be telling of our times to be
when tide and moon are at their height;
I have been dreaming half the night
of holding you beside the sea
and watching waves crash into light.

The Short English Madrigal follows the same rhyming pattern
and system of repetitions as the Madrigal proper, but is in lines of
iambic tetrameter (˘ ′ ˘ ′ ˘ ′ ˘ ′).

M A D S O N G   S T A N Z A

In Dusk

When the blood of the setting sun
stains both trees and sky
and the last bird
is no longer heard
I hear the earth sigh

for just the smallest moment
as sharp leaves stir
in the little wind,
a gentle, kind
cool breath of air

a contemplative man might think
made by some ghost
allowed at last
to relive the past,
grieve to the uttermost,

save that as dusk descends
there's no sense of true grief;
it rather seems
a time for dreams
for loosened bonds, for relief,

and if ghosts wander here
remembering days gone
they ease the heart
by sharing part
of the journey we travel on.

The Madsong Stanza as defined by Lewis Turco, who relates it to the medieval cuckoo song and to Tom O'Bedlam's Song, is in podic verse, sometimes called stress verse or sprung rhythm. This is to say that the verse is based upon the stressed syllable count only, and unstressed syllables are not considered. The stress count for the five line stanza is 3 3 2 2 3 and the rhyme scheme is A B C C B.

POULTERS MEASURE

Crow Messge

I do not wholly trust the crow upon the wall;
its yellow eye pretends to truth, but does not tell it all.

It hides beneath its claw a fragmentary fact
that, were his greed to let it go, would make all things
        exact,

and logic would be ruler of all our thoughts and deeds;

no idle fancies would exist, no isms and no creeds,

or so his eye suggests, that wicked yellow eye;
I beg him not to lift his claw until I have gone by.

Poulters Measure consists of a couplet, the first line being an iambic hexameter or alexandrine, and the second being an iambic heptameter or fourteener. The second line should have a break after the eighth syllable, and the couplet should rhyme. If the couplet is relineated as a quatrain, it becomes Short Measure.

P R I M E R   C O U P L E T S

Crow on a Bough

The perching crow
sees us below
his chosen bough
but can't allow
our right to stand
here on the land
his blackness claims;
he calls us names,
recounts our sins
and then begins
to sneer and curse
and, what is worse,
to tease and mock.
I throw a rock
and make his day.
He squawks away.

The Primer Couplet consists of two rhyming lines each of which contain two stressed syllables. The metre may be mixed.

R I M E   R O Y A L

S a m h a i n   I n   P e r u g i a

To climb these streets is not to meet the dead
as people say, but rather to be met.
Stone streets encompass us; a horn-crowned head
surveys us, mocking, from its parapet.
Words enter us and ask for answers, yet
no language can respond; we pause before
a set of steps up to an ancient door.

Are we supposed to enter? Should we knock
or lift the iron ring in that grim jaw?
Surely we need some great key for that lock?
The plaque set in the wall seems destined for
a time ahead of ours; although, before
we came here, we supposed ourselves at ease
in this, the latest of our centuries.

We are less certain now. This twisted stair
is one more journey we have always known,
this well a depth of dark we questioned where
and who and when before we were full grown,
the cobbled square a meeting place. We own
so little and so much; we cannot tell
if this is madness or a miracle.

And yet in the piazza, watching how

the fountain plays on in the fading light,
the dead that have encountered us allow
that we and they, in this and every night,
are sharing earth; dreams hover, land, take flight,
their dreams our dreams, their ways our ways, all one,
and time left shiftless on the climbing stone.

Rime Royal is a stanza form composed of seven, ten syllable lines with the rhyme scheme A B A B B C C. The metre is iambic pentameter, but is usually treated with considerable freedom as here. The basic formula is ˘ ′ ˘ ′ ˘ ′ ˘ ′ ˘ ′ .

ROUNDEL

The Hand

You touched my hand, then took the touch away;
as if a falling leaf had chanced to land
upon a stone and chosen not to stay
you touched my hand.

But it was more than leaf; it trembled and
it was as if some creature gone astray
sought for a place that it could understand.

I did not speak. What was there I could say?
I merely glanced down at your fingers and
somehow, inevitably, as if planned,
you touched my hand.

The Roundel has no set metre. It consists of eleven lines in three stanzas. The first part of the first line being repeated at the end of the first stanza and at the conclusion of the whole. This half line also forms part of the rhyme scheme. It is here given a large capital A: A B B A B A * A B A * B A B A

Tether's End

Here's the mailman with a letter:
what if it should be from her?
I already am her debtor,
she incomparably fair;
I'm unable to forget her;
this is more that I can bear.

I already am her debtor,
she incomparably fair;
how did I contrive to get her
to engage in this affaire?
I'm unable to forget her;
this is more than I can bear.

How did I contrive to get her
to engage in this affaire?
Did our stars combine to let her

snare me in her golden hair?
I'm unable to forget her;
this is more than I can bear.

Did our stars combine to let her
snare me in her golden hair,
teach her how to chain and fetter
men that kiss before they care?
I'm unable to forget her;
this is more that I can bear.

The Roundelay, as a specific verse form rather than a general term for a lyric carrying a refrain, was invented by Dryden. The metre is trochaic tetrameter ($\prime\smile\prime\smile\prime\smile\prime\smile$), some of the lines being *catalectic* (i.e. one syllable short) to ensure a strong concluding rhyme. The rhyme scheme of each of the four stanzas is A B A B A B. The lines are repeated in a given order, thus: 1 2 3 4 5 6 * 3 4 7 8 5 6 * 7 8 9 10 5 6 * 9 10 11 12 5 6. This formula could be expressed in terms of line pairs thus: 1 2 3 * 2 4 3 * 4 5 3 * 5 6 3.

ENGLISH RUBAI _____

Maya

Illusion is the only word we know;
what's shown to us is nothing more than show,
and when it's finished and the house-lights on
guess and belief, abandoned, turn and go.

The English Rubai was created by Fitzgerald in his *Rubaiyat of Omar Khayyam*. It is derived from the Persian Rubai, which is a quatrain rhyming A A B A and a poem in itself. Fitzgerald retained the Persian rhyme scheme but changed the metre to iambic pentameter ($\smile\prime\ \smile\prime\ \smile\prime\ \smile\prime\ \smile\prime$) and strung his quatrains together to form a sequence.

Night Vision

I have no quarrel with the night,
for it is only in the light
I see the threadbare and the wan
that face the day with failing sight

and wander, aimless, one by one,
as if there's nothing to be done
but bear the deadweight of their needs
beneath the vastness of the sun

that neither notices nor heeds
the tyranny that starves and bleeds
the homeless hunched beneath the sky,
but looks upon all mortal deeds

with equal and impervious eye,
and only when the shadows lie
long on the sidewalks and, behind
the buildings, day begins to die,

can I, blindfolded by the kind
all-healing darkness, fill my mind
with echoes of that ancient thought
that fantasized a world designed

for more than greed's malicious sport,
but such philosophies are naught
when I again am shamed by light.
I have no quarrel with the night.

The interlocking Rubaiyat is composed in lines of eight or ten syllables with the rhyme scheme A A B A as in Fitzgerald's *Rubaiyat of Omar Khayam*. The B rhyme of one verse becomes the A rhyme of the next and so on until the last stanza when there may or may not be a variation as in the above.

SHORT HYMNAL STANZA

The Street

The face across the street
is one I daily see
where patterned curtains fail to meet;
it sometimes stares at me.

It sometimes gazes out
of that small private place;
the eyes are wide with fear and doubt
as it surveys my face,

I tug my curtains closed.
I do not wish to see
my own despair and pain exposed
to rancid loyalty,

nor do I dare to think
that shape of wax and bone

that peers out from the curtains chink
could almost be my own,

that we each brought a name
from birthwords of the past
that bring the curse of death and shame
as long as small streets last.

Short Hymnal Measure consists of quatrains in iambic (‿ ́) metre
with the syllable count 6 6 8 6 and the rhyme scheme A B A B. Short
Measure differs from it only in having the rhyme scheme A B C B.

SHORT PARTICULAR MEASURE

Birch

Lucidities
of silver trees
with slim and turning leaves
bless and release
the day to peace
and soothe the heart that grieves.

Free to the air
the branches stir
and sway as if in dreams
without a care
that all may share
who see the thin leaves' gleams

that come and go
and ebb and flow,

a life-enhancing breeze
that calms us so
that we may know
lucidities of trees.

The Short Particular Measure consists of six-line stanzas the first,
second, fourth and fifth lines being iambic trimeter (˘ ´ ˘ ´ ˘ ´)
and the third and sixth lines being iambic tetrameter (˘ ´ ˘ ´ ˘ ´
˘ ´). The rhyme scheme is A A B A A B.

S K E L T O N I C S _____

The Hidden

This log has stayed
in the tangled glade
for a full year
of my walking here.
Then yesterday,
partly in play,
I gave it a push:
it rolled over in a rush
and my heart was shaken
to see brown shapes waken,
scuttling to hide
from the day they'd been denied
in the log's darkened house -

grammarsows
in a scurrying herd.
I could find no word
to calm their fright;
they were in full flight
back into night.
What could I write
of that sad sight,
creatures running from light
as if it were a blight,
a mortal attack?
I rolled the log back
afraid there were
hard lessons there.

Skeltonics, named after the poet John Skelton (1460-1529) are rhymed podic verses, which is to say that only the stressed syllables are taken into account. There are either two or three stressed syllables in each Skeltonic line and occasionally four and the lines are rhymed together in couplets, triplets, or even larger groups.

CAUDATE SONNET

After Long Absense

Am I remembered? Does my name recall
anything but a shadowy sort of thing,

someone leaning up against a wall,
one of the faces at a launch or reading,
perhaps a string of letters on the spine
of something sometime read but put aside,
lost to a long ago that once was mine,
or partly mine. They cannot all have died
though some have slithered off I understand.
Obituaries make their sluggish way
across a sea, a continent, fulsome, bland.
Sometimes I think to write, but words won't play.
Do you remember what I almost can't?
As ghost I'm much too insecure to haunt,
although I'd wish to flaunt
my distant eminence, give my work its due,
I fear that testy unresponsive *Who?*

The Caudate Sonnet is a sonnet with a tail composed of one short line which rhymes with a preceding line in the sonnet and usually the fourteenth, and a rhyming couplet in iambic pentameter. Any sonnet form may be used; the above is a Shakespearean sonnet.

CURTAL SONNET

Slow Music

For Murray Adaskin

It is the slower music stirs the mind,
each heard note a footfall felt and known,
a comprehension of the weight of things
and an insistence that we stumble, blind
with seeing, and through hearing must be shown,

sound by deep sound, the pulsebeat of time's wings.

We must be taught to guard within our hoard
each warp and woof of measure and of tone,
all dooms and glories of heart's wanderings
surpassing price, and bow to that last chord
Death brings.

This variation on the Sonnet form was created by Gerard Manley Hopkins. It has eleven lines instead of fourteen. The syllable count is: 10 10 10 10 10 10 * 10 10 10 10 2. The end rhymes are: A B C A B C D B C D C. The rhythmic pattern has ten lines of iambic pentameter followed by one line composed of a single spondee.

SHAKESPEAREAN SONNET

The Biographers

In Memoriam Richard Ciccimarra (1924-1973)

The story that they tell is one of wives
successively acquired, discarded, blamed,
of his three separate fascinating lives:
the quiet drunkard's, solitary, shamed;
the fisherman's, rod curving to the streams,
remote with skill; the artist's (last of all),
a life of silhouettes and dwindling dreams,

an endless angst pinned to his spinning wall.

They almost never tell of hours of thought,
of his unnerving vision of mankind,
those taut and piercing purities that caught
the infinite stillness at the edge of mind,
nor how his fine line drew up from the deep
these watchful presences that haunt our sleep.

The Shakespearean Sonnet is in iambic pentameter, and broken
into two parts, an octet and a sestet, thus being fourteen lines in
toto. The metre is ˘ ´ ˘ ´ ˘ ´ ˘ ´ ˘ ´. The rhyme scheme is: A B
A B C D C D * E F E F G G.

SPENSERIAN SONNET

Ghost Story

For Jean Kozokari

They noticed that she never closed a door
but always left it open just a bit.
They asked her what on earth she did it for.
She told them very seriously "It
is for my cat." They almost had a fit;
there was no cat in view. They asked her "Where?

We see no cat!" She said, "It's gone to sit
upon the cretonned sofa over there."
Her parents clutched their temples in despair.
The child was crazy. What were they to do?
This fantasy was more than they could bear.
She said "I'm sorry, but I thought you knew.
It drowned. It has been drowned for several weeks."
She rather liked the rhythm of their shrieks.

The Spenserian Sonnet consists of fourteen lines of iambic pentameter (˘ ʹ ˘ ʹ ˘ ʹ ˘ ʹ ˘ ʹ) with the rhyme scheme A B A B B
C B C C D C D E E. It is named after Edmund Spenser who invented
the form.

SPENSERIAN STANZA
_____

A n i m a

The shadow of a standing woman, grey
with presence, watches from my study door,
as if solidity; I cannot say
who she may be or what she's asking for,
or should I say commanding? There's no law
tells me I must submit, and yet she seems
more strong than all authority and more
aware of all my stratagems and schemes,
the guide and governess of my dark unspoken dreams.

What must I do? She shapes no word or sound

or even gesture, but stands stiff and still
as if carved out of time's half darkness, bound
by neither night nor day, but by the skill
of something, someone other to fulfill
a task. Am I that task? There's no reply,
but as I ask I know that shadow will
not leave me in this life, and when I die
will be the light I learn my further journey by.

The Spenserian Stanza, so called because it is used by Spenser in
The Faerie Queene, consists of nine lines, the first eight being in
iambic pentameter and the ninth having an additional iambic foot.
The rhyme scheme is A B A B B C B C C.

SPLIT COUPLET

Leaf

There's this one leaf upon the tree.
It troubles me.

It is the last leaf left, up high,
withered and dry.

I think somehow it ought to claim
a prophet's name,

a lonely prophet, gaunt and wild,
unloved, reviled,

but now it breaks off and in flight
is feather-light,

the last frail dancer on our boards,
The earth applauds.

The split couplet is composed of two lines, the first having eight
syllables, the second four. The metre is iambic and runs ˘ ´ ˘ ´ ˘ ´
˘ ´ * ˘ ´ ˘ ´. The lines should rhyme with each other.

TRIVERSEN
_____

The Hill

Under the hill
  behind the village
    lie ancestral bones.

We rarely speak of them,
  would not disturb them
    with our voices.

However, at the year's turn
  when dry leaves fall
    we pay them a visit.

We ask them nothing,
  tell them little

but offer blessings.

Once in a while
   mist makes shapes on the hill
     and we smile on our children.

We tell our children
   "Feel safe;
     you are never alone."

The Triversen Stanza originated with William Carlos Williams. There is no syllable count or required metre. Each stanza consists of three lines, each line being a distinct clause or phrase in a sentence that is complete within the stanza. Ideally, the whole poem should have six stanzas.

TRISYLLABICS

Brentwood

Down the track
between the
thinking trees

what is it
travelling
inner space

with such deep
certainty?
It is not

visible
to any
human eye

but only
what we call
a presence

having no
sure term or
any time

to think it
out and say
it's only

how we walk
ourselves when
truth is near.

Trisyllabics are simply lines of verse composed in three syllables.

T U D O R   L Y R I C

Marsh Cottage Revisited

This grey morning,
the sky turning
to red warning,
my dawn recalls
a barren meadow

still in shadow,
a torn hedgerow,
crumbling walls,

a land dying,
the wind crying
and rain sighing
through warped trees
on a drab coast
and there, a ghost,
I face a host
of memories;

each loneliness
and each distress
and long sickness
is gathered here
where once, alone,
something unknown
brought me my own
and special fear,

the fear that I
may never die
nor get to lie
at last in rest
but must go on
and on and on
till Time, undone,
says *Satis Est.*

This lyric form appears a number of times in late fifteenth century manuscripts and was also used by Wyatt. The lines have two stresses each and four syllables, the rhyme scheme of each eight line stanza being A A A B C C C B. There is no general agreement on metre, but the majority of the lines are iambic (˘ ´) or trochaic (´ ˘). It is a variation of the Welsh Long Rhupunt and probably came into English verse by way of the Welsh speakers in the Tudor court.

Viator I

Dover Beach Revisited

As shingle slides upon the shore
this gentle summer night, we stroll,
the great bear pointing to the pole
as if to prove what stars are for.

A far light winks once then is gone
as shingle slides upon the shore;
impermanence we know is law
and, hand in hand, we wander on

bemused by moonlight on the sea
and troubled by a distant war;
as shingle slides upon the shore
I turn to you and you to me

and though, above, the jet-planes roar,
the universe has come to be
a moon that's mirrored in the sea
as shingle slides upon the shore.

The Viator is my own invention, and consists of any stanzaic poem in which the first line of the first stanza is the second line of the second stanza and so on until the poem ends with the line with which it began. The name *Viator* is the latin for traveller.

Aging

Though I grow old,
(hair turning white),
stiff-boned and cold

I take delight
(though I grow old)
in all that's bright

and strong and bold
and praise the light,
though I grow old.

Evening

Once the summer day is done
and darkness moves in from the sea
to brush us with oblivion,
and twilight, sly with mystery,
spreads shadows where the sun has shone
I'm troubled by eternity.

Thoughts of Time's ending come to me
once the summer day is done
and moments grow and change to be
hour-long or suddenly are gone.

I'm troubled by eternity,
this one life travelling on and on.

The rising moon denies the sun,
and stars trace out their destiny
once the summer day is done;
I'm troubled by eternity,
the signature within my bone
that shapes another name for me,

a name that spells inexorably
all I have been, each thread I've spun.
I'm troubled by eternity
once the summer day is done,
for subtle twilight turns the key
to unlock dreams I've trampled on,

revive desires I've learned to shun.
I'm troubled by eternity
exhuming every skeleton
in my ridiculous history.
Once the summer day is done
night whispers perpetuity.

I'm troubled by eternity,
that unexplored dominion
of everyone's entirety,
no episode omitted, none.
Night whispers perpetuity
once the summer day is done.

The Double Viator consists of six, six-line stanzas, the first line of
the first stanza becoming the second one of the second and so forth,
while the last line of the sixth stanza becomes the penultimate line
of the fifth, and so forth. The rhyme scheme of the first two stanzas is A B A B A B   B A B A B A; this is repeated three times.

ETHIOPIAN

Felinity

For Neile Graham

Watching round-eyed kittens
   crouched small to pounce, waylay,
under the garden shed,
   I'm clear meat can't allay
that hunter hunger, quick
   to flex curved claws and play
the dancing killing game
   that ends with a display
of death on threshold stone,
   yet, weighing their outlay
of leap and grab and shake,
   it seems a sad melee —
scuffle, squeak, limp silence —
   still, Nature daren't delay
or thwart that judging claw
   or spare the limbs that splay
out on the death-smeared step;
   clay must return to clay.

Mawaddes is the name of a nine line poem usually composed in hexameters with a strong caesura halfway through. There is only one rhyming sound in the poem and it concludes all the lines. The rhymes are made up of identical consonant + vowel combinations. The vowel + consonant formula is not acceptable. This verse form is found in the Ge'ez language and ceased to be used at the end of the eighteenth century.

FINNISH

Cavern

Where the coast road turned a corner
opposite the gorse-gold bushes,
boyhood found a blackthorn cavern
in the darkly tangled hedgerow;
there I'd squat small, think of nothing,
feel myself completely severed
from the sunlit passing cycles,
clopping horses, strolling couples.
Disregarding all that happened
in the shining world outside me
I became not boy but creature
hunched in private secret knowledge.

Could it be that some ancestral
even stone-age mind persisted
in the cool dark of the hedgerow?
Could it be Fate had returned me
to the womb to find lost secrets?
Even, maybe, hedgehogs, foxes,
blackbirds, yellow-hammers, sparrows
had left sounds and scents behind them
to transfigure and possess me.

Who can tell? And yet I wonder
when time shows me I am dying
will I not for one brief moment

find myself in that cool cavern,
womb-round, animal, ancestral,
find it, as I almost found it
in my boyhood, a dark tunnel
to a light I'd left behind me.

The Kalevala metre is composed in lines of eight syllables containing four stresses, the final syllable of each line being unstressed. The metre was used by Longfellow for *Hiawatha*, though he also used the Hebrew verse principle of Parallelismus Membrorum.

FRENCH

Changes

The old man watches from the chair
he made two centuries ago;
none but myself can see him there
or that his hand is moving, slow
as destiny, opening to show
me once again a disc of bone
engraved with a black hooded crow;
time alters when we lie alone.

Solitary dreamers dare
to balk the current of life's flow,
tread water, breathe a different air,
and, caught up in the long ago,
find how our yesterdays may grow
from our tomorrows, the unknown
shape certainties we dare not know;
time alters when we lie alone;

it draws clawed combs through golden hair
and hides a depthless well below
the threshold of a winding stair;
it spills red blood upon the snow;
it guides us where our memories go
and cuts our names and years in stone.
However brightly histories glow,

time alters when we lie alone.

The old man's gone, yet, poised just so,
black on the scarred and empty throne
a feather trembles to and fro;
time alters when we lie alone.

The Ballade is composed of three stanzas of eight lines and one of four called an envoy or envoi. There is no rule as to line length or metre, but eight syllable and ten syllable lines are the most frequent and iambs (˘ ´) are the usual feet. The rhyme scheme is as follows, the last line of each stanza being a refrain: A B A B B C B C * A B A B B C B C * A B A B B C B C * B C B C.

DOUBLE REFRAIN BALLADE

Night Thoughts: Bosnia

We walk outside and, craning, stare;
above black roofs the planets soar.
Do these, our constellations, care?
Can there be love within the law?
Back in the cushioned house once more
we watch the screen, see cities where
the one remaining word is War
as deaths of children choke the air.

Fear bloodies all the oaths men swear
and Freedom's lifted hand's a claw
while Nationhood strips mountains bare.
Can there be love within the law?
Or in the sights of those that score

direct hits upon school and square,
re-opening history's darkest door
as deaths of children choke the air?

What should we do? How can we spare
the time to grieve, to judge? Before
we act there's laws we must prepare.
Can there be love within the law?
Statutes could stumble. What is more
their loyalties are their own affair
and Pride has heroes to adore
as deaths of children choke the air.

Outside the planets burn and soar.
Can there be love within the law?
What is this universe we share
as deaths of children choke the air?

The Double Refrain Ballade differs from the Ballade Proper in making the fourth line of each stanza a refrain as well as the eighth. The envoi consists of a quatrain rhyming in couplets. The usual rhyme scheme of each stanza is A B A B b c B C. I have chosen the stricter scheme of A B A B b b b A B A. Thus my envoi rhymes b B A A instead of b B c C.

BALLADE SUPREME
_____

Discoveries

Hair of copper, eyes of green,
level-browed she faced me there
en route to school. That pinning stare

cost me my breath, brought me aware
that taboos of the rigid law
could break and crumble. Awed before
the shock, I stumbled on the track
and knew the opening of a door.
No god can call the lightning back.

Days may break suddenly, each clean
division showing truths one dare
not claim as wisdom for they mean
as do first snowflakes, diamonds' flare,
a shooting star, the shine of hair,
a sunlit patch on polished floor;
one time it happened on the shore —
I found within the bladderwrack
a pebble breathing like a spore.
No god can call the lightning back.

It may be all the lives I've been
were nothing more than puffs of air
ephemeral to the changing scene,
or did they climb an endless stair
as do I, constantly, and bear
the very burdens that they bore?
Each life relearns a timeless lore,
yet once I heard the great tree crack,
and, as the bough fell, watched birds soar.
No god can call the lightning back.

My grandson crawls upon the floor,
each moment adding to his store
of revelations some new knack,
the wonderment that time is for.
No god can call the lightning back.

The Ballade Supreme consists of three ten line stanzas and a five
line envoi. The stanzas have the rhyme scheme A B A B B C C D C D
and the envoi C C D C D. The refrain line of the above is an adapta-
tion of a line by William Stafford, "Even God can't take the lightning back."

Two other variations of the Ballade are the Double Ballade and
the Double Ballade Supreme. As these differ from the usual only
in having twice the usual number of stanzas, I have not included
them.

BREF DOUBLE

Downfall

For Charles Lillard

They've trucked the stones away;
there's little to be seen
but wrecked shrubs, trampled grass
where human history stood

foursquare, a solid fact;
one broken sheet of glass
is shining at the sun
because it thinks it should;

trees, drably ill at ease,
look half inclined to pray
as if grouped round a grave
here in the puddled mud

but what can old trees say?
They have seen centuries pass.

The Bref Double, like the sonnet, has fourteen lines and can, therefore, be called a quatorzain. It does, however, have a definite rhyme
scheme, though there is no restriction as to line length or metre.
There are three rhymes in the poem but also unrhymed lines. The
rhyme scheme runs: A - B C * - B - C * -A - C * A B. This is the
formula given by Lewis Turco.

CHANT ROYAL

Serena

There is a pause before full night
when the familiar grows unknown,
the mirror shining more than bright,
the vase of flowers carved in stone.
Though everything is in its place
something has twisted time and space
and it's as if a blurring veil
has moved aside so that the pale
and ordinary gains a shine
of pride; as daylight starts to fail
the edge of evening whispers wine.

It's then we understand how sight
may be a blindness; we are shown
this colour, that, think black, think white,
observe the shapes of wood and stone,
examine artifacts and trace
their histories, fumble silk and lace,
weigh them on our aesthetic scale,
but it is as the blind use braille
to bring them an unseen design.
When day's perceptions dull and stale

the edge of evening whispers wine.

It's more with wonder than delight
that we feel strangeness in the bone
on facing change. One can take fright
when, standing in this dusk alone,
one feels that one is keeping pace
with something, someone, in a race
along an undiscovered trail
towards a distant mythic grail,
a dream that guilt dare not decline,
a lifted cup that histories hail;
the edge of evening whispers wine.

We shrug this off as well we might;
it's not our business to atone
for ancient ills, share any rite
or pilgrimage, for we have grown
beyond such fantasies; we face
our days with reason and embrace
no tales of unicorn or whale,
of rose or thorn or speaking gale,
incredulous of every sign —
yet sometimes all convictions quail:
the edge of evening whispers wine.

Not day, not night, these hours excite
us in a manner we've not known
since childhood when we thought the height
of truth was magic on a throne.
Now older, colder, we disgrace
those dreams by scurrying to chase
a vogue, a name, a prize, a sale
though at the last they don't avail;
when instinct, thought and sense combine
to challenge reason and prevail

the edge of evening whispers wine.

Now that the light is thin and frail
let's sieze the moment to curtail
crude reason's rule and countermine
the strictures of the daily tale —
the edge of evening whispers wine.

The Chant Royal usually has lines of eight or ten syllables and is composed in iambic tetrameter or pentameter. There are five stanzas of eleven lines each and one of five which is termed the envoi or envoy. There is a refrain. The rhyme scheme is as follows. The first four stanzas have the pattern A B A B C C D D E D E, each stanza using the same rhyme sounds. The envoy has the rhyme scheme D D E D E.

Dizain

At Goldstream

Here salmon swim with birth and death
back to the pools where both were bred,
renewing life with each trapped breath;
broken, tattered, bleeding red
upon the rippling river bed
they spill their seed as do we all
who, dying, leap a waterfall
to our eternal origin,
and though the seeds are few and small
they are the lives our deaths begin.

The Dizain is a poem of ten lines of eight or ten syllables each, the

metre being iambic tetrameter or pentameter. The rhyme scheme
is A B A B B C C D C D.

Unsurprising

In the bare space between the rocks
I find a footprint in the sand,
small, sharp-edged, delicate; it looks
as if a wandering child had found
the rock-bound route a failure and
decided not to chance a leap,
lacking the needful helpful hand;
the earth turns over in its sleep.

The broken door is gaping wide
and there is no sound, none at all.
I take a breath and edge inside;
the Van Gogh sunflowers in the hall
stare at chairs, table, sideboard, all
abandoned, lost. The stairs are steep
and one bed cowers to the wall.
The earth turns over in its sleep.

She turns to me; her eyes are dazed
and her mouth trembles as she sighs,
half gripped by grief and half amazed;
how dare the usual day surprise
her love by laying bare such lies.
Her hand is cold. She will not weep.

Pride furnishes a fresh disguise;
the earth turns over in its sleep.

The Huitain may either be a poem in itself or, as here, a stanza. It is composed in an eight or ten syllable line with the rhyme scheme A B A B B C B C. The metre is usually iambic (˘ ´). It is also called the Monk's Tale Stanza because Chaucer used it; Villon also used it very frequently. The refrain is not necessary. Another rhyme scheme is A B B A A C A C.

K Y R I E L L E I

Portrait Of An Unknown Lady

Head poised beneath its weight of hair,
eyes that could be God's comforter
and hands that make a hymn of bone:
I long to know what won't be known.

No priestess could shine out as proud
and separate from the jostling crowd
or seem so candidly alone;
I long to know what won't be known.

Remote as tides' horizons, she
boasts neither name nor history;
we only see what we are shown.
I long to know what won't be known

until, time ending, all comes clear.
Her gown's the music of the weir
that slides and hides the changeless stone;

I long to know what won't be known,

at one with all the human race
that cries out in each sacred place
where timeless mysteries have grown,
"I long to know what won't be known."

Any rhymed quatrains with last lines in common may be termed a
Kyrielle according to Gleeson White's authoritative essay of 1887.
He, himself, gave a rhyme scheme of A A B B as in this example,
there being eight syllables in each line.

KYRIELLE II

Cornish Summer

For John Knight

In West Penwith as time slides on
we learn how coming years may lie
of who we were and what was done.
History passes history by.

The ruined tin mines of Lelant
now stretch black fingers to the sky
where Cornish preachers used to rant.
History passes history by.

Its healing rivulets run dry,
the holy well at Madron's grown
a welter of mud, thorn and stone.
History passes history by.

Half broken, leaning on the land
that poles and pylons dignify
upon the moor stone circles stand.
History passes history by.

The past is past, forgotten, done;
we question neither when nor why
as, lounging in the summer sun,
History passes history by.

This Kyrielle uses the rhyme scheme proposed by Lewis Turco in
The New Book of Forms and is A B A B.

K Y R I E L L E   I I I
_____

G o n e   A w a y

Now that you have gone away
and I no longer watch you dance
the street to some great new romance
there is no music in the day.

The cliche's true. Life was a play
in which you took a carefree part.
I lack the skill to learn that art;
there is no music in the day.

Lost love's a phrase I will not use;
it would be an absurdity;
I simply say that now, for me,
there is no music in the day.

It is less tragedy than dismay;
I should have known it from the past;
when lasting pleasures fail to last
there is no music in the day.

The rhyme scheme of this Kyrielle is A B B A.

On the Coast

In this grove of trees
    all realities
        lose way
as mist off the sea's
    infinity frees
        the day
from its certainties,
    bringing fantasies,
        mind-play.

As distinctions end
    and the mists descend
        and drift,
leaf-harmonies blend
    in a dance, extend
        and shift
their shapes, pretend
    illusions portend
        some gift.

We dream it may be
  the ability
    to find
  our heredity
  in earth's mystery
    of mind,
but mist drifts off; we
  see what we must see,
    still blind.

The Lai is a poem or a stanza with a definite syllable count and rhyme scheme, though there is no metrical restriction.
    Syllables: 5 5 2 5 5 2 5 5 2
    Rhymes: A A B A A B A A B

L A I N O U V E A U

Song For Beltaine I

Dear one, take my hand.
Love is what is planned
today.
Brightness fills the land
and, at her command,
white May
trembles petals and
joy strikes up the band.

None can countermand
such laws, or withstand,
suppress
song or saraband.

She has cast out, banned
distress.
Love is what is planned.
Dear one, take my hand.

The Lai Nouveau is composed in stanzas of eight lines. The first
line is repeated as the last line of the second stanza, the second line
as the last line of the third stanza, and so forth. The poem ends
with a repetition of the first two lines of the poem in reverse order.
Syllables:　5 5 2 5 5 2 5 5
Rhymes:　A A B A A B A A

O D E (R O N S A R D ' S F O R M)

At Sunset, Waiting

If you were meant to come here you will know
as well as I;
if you were meant to sit beside me here
and watch the sky
turn very slowly pink, then red, and shine
with all the flushed complaisance of spilt wine,
you'll understand
that it was planned
by other minds than yours or mine.

What shapes these meetings no one can explain
or even guess,
yet now, as dark descends and the last stain
fades and is less
a splendour than a memory of pride,
I'm almost sure I feel you by my side

having come far,
yet who you are
is knowledge I have been denied.

Is this the same experience for you?
Was there a choice?
Are you, bathed in the sunset, waiting too
for a new voice
speaking this way or in some other fashion,
perhaps gently, perhaps strained with passion,
someone unknown?
Am I alone
in suffering this obsession?

Darkness is here and you are not, although
I have a sense
of someone reaching out to me, and so
it's no pretence,
and staring up at this first evening star
I know wherever we may think we are
we are now, here,
apart and near,
for time has no such thought as far.

The Ronsardian Ode is the only ode form that has definite rules. Petrarchan Odes can take many shapes and the English Ode is never consistently one form even when practiced by its supposed master, Keats. The Ronsardian Ode is composed in an undetermined number of nine-line stanzas.

Syllable count is: 10 4 10 4 10 10 4 4 8
Rhyme scheme: A B A B C C D D C

In An Abandoned Cemetery

Though once a mason spelled them out
these lifetimes now are lost, unknown;
masking both certainty and doubt,
slow moss has covered up the stone.

These lifetimes now are lost, unknown;
the years have hidden each carved word;
slow moss has covered up the stone;
no single letter has been spared.

The years have hidden each carved word
as we have every personal shame;
no single letter has been spared,
no smallest vestige of a name.

As we have every personal shame
these green slabs have concealed the past,
no smallest vestige of a name,
no sometime fame allowed to last.

These green slabs have concealed the past,
renouncing love and pain and pride,
no sometime fame allowed to last,
all mortal dignity denied.

Renouncing love and pain and pride
slow moss has covered up the stone,
all mortal dignity denied;
these lifetimes now are lost, unknown.

Slow moss have covered up the stone,
masking both certainty and doubt;
these lifetimes now are lost, unknown
though once a mason spelled them out.

The Pantoum has no fixed number of syllables. It is in rhyming quatrains with the end rhyme pattern A B A B. The second and fourth lines of one stanza are repeated as the first and third lines of the one following. The last stanza may be either a couplet composed of the first and third lines of the whole in reversed order, or a quatrain with these lines taking the second and fourth positions.

Some versions have the Pantoum ending with the second and fourth lines of the first stanza taking the second and fourth places once again, only in reverse order.

A short Pantoum could be expressed in the following formula, using capital letters for the repeated rhyming lines, and numerals to distinguish between those lines: A1 B1 A2 B2 * B1 C1 B2 C2 * C1 D1 C2 D2 * and, as the last stanza D1 A2 D2 A1 or D1 B2 D2 B1 or, simply, A2 A1.

The Pantoum ideally should have two themes, one carried by the first two lines of each quatrain and one by the second two.

The metre is according to choice.

The Pantoum was developed from the Malaysian Pantun by Victor Hugo, and differs considerably from its original.

RONDEAU

Full Moon

The moon's at full. Our bedroom's bright
as shutters cast their bars of light
on wall and bed and floor. You slide
out from our sheets, throw shutters wide

and stand there as if planning flight,

staring so fixedly one might
almost imagine wings spread white
up from your shoulders, poised to glide.
The moon's at full.

I fear for you, as well I might,
for it is dangerous to invite
such freedom, yet love can't provide
love more than love where love may hide....
The moon's at full.

The Rondeau has no rules concerning metre or line length. It consists of three sections of five, four, and six lines respectively, the first half of the first line being repeated as the last line of the second and third sections. The rhyme scheme is as follows, the letter R denoting the repeated half line: R A B B A * A A B R * A A B B A R. The line length most commonly used is eight or ten syllables.

RONDEAU REDOUBLE

Spring In The Okanagan

For Kerry Slavens

The river rose a good foot more today.
I murmur 'run-off' but the terror grows.
It could move closer, wash the past away;
when time is ready that's the way it goes.

Way high upon the watching hemlock crows

have gathered as if waiting for their prey,
for floods mean carrion everybody knows.
The river rose a good foot more today;

it's lapping at my garden. Will it stay,
swell, spread, and grow more turbulent? I suppose
this could be just a passing small display.
I murmur 'run-off' but the terror grows.

I can't help wondering if my tension shows.
Comfortingly all the neighbors say
it won't be very long before it goes.
It could move closer, wash the past away,

suck at foundations till walls tilt and sway
and tumble, doomed by distant melting snows.
However we prepare, or watch and pray
when time is ready that's the way it goes —

at first a rippling wave or two, in play
it seems, but then strong darker waves expose
the message: destiny is on its way.
Today, annihilating all repose,
the river rose.

The Rondeau Redouble consists of five quatrains and a sixth concluding stanza with five lines, the last line being the first part of
the first line of all. The first four lines of the poem form refrain
lines in turn for the following four stanzas. The formula could be
expressed thus: A1 B1 A2 B2 * b a b A1 * a b a B1 * b a b A2
* a b a B2 * b a b a ½ A1.

The Visitation

You touched my fingers and you smiled
and then there was no world but you,
no guests, no party, nothing new
or old, but you remote and wild

and yet familiar, gentle, mild,
one sadness took its troubles to;
you touched my fingers and you smiled
and then there was no world but you.

I was bewitched, enslaved, beguiled;
whatever was most false, most true,
came all together and I knew
it was because I was your child
you touched my fingers and you smiled.

The Rondel is a thirteen line poem divided into three stanzas of four, four, and five lines respectively. The first line is repeated as the seventh and the final line. The second line is repeated as the eighth line. The rhyme scheme is thus: A B b a * a b A B * a b b a A.

Methusalah's Song

I never planned
on growing old
but now the cold
chills heart and hand,

and I can't stand
the lies I'm told
I never planned
on growing old,

white-haired, unmanned,
and losing hold;
the years were gold
with promise and
I never planned
on growing old.

The Rondel Supreme has the end rhyme pattern A B B A * A B A B * A B B A A B. There are no restrictions as to syllable count or metre.

Grandmother: A Portrait In Petit Point

For Roy Skelton

I can't forget
the creak of that opening door.
   I can't forget
the narrow thread of light, nor yet
the slide of her skirt on the floor,
her goodnight cheek; and there is more
   I can't forget —

   such minor things —
the papery skin of her face —
   such minor things,
her knuckles, her big heavy rings,
her necklace of jet, her lace;
why does childhood memory trace
   such minor things?

   Is she no more
than this — a collection of scraps?
   Is she no more
than the opening of that door,
an old gentle face, and perhaps
a perfume that memory grasps?
   Is she no more?

The Rondelet is a seven line poem or stanza, the first line reappearing as the third and seventh. The syllable count being 4 8 4 8 8 8 4 and the pattern of endrhymes A b A a b b A.

Night Watch

Still, listening, as she breathes beside me here,
I think her wandering whitely and alone
through golden deserts fringed by towers of stone;
the little breaths that happen at my ear
are moths that flutter sunward without fear
while I lie in a darkness all my own,
still listening.

Some night a single dream-shed word may clear
away that darkness, show what she's been shown,
and I will know what she has always known
when, darkness done, I lie beside her here,
still listening.

The Rondine is a twelve line poem divided into two parts, one of seven and one of five lines. The opening words of the first line form the seventh and twelfth lines and are refrains (R). Thus the rhyme scheme may be given as: Ra b b a a b R * a b b a R.

There is no rule as to line length or metre.

SPONDAIC TRIOLET

Lullaby For Veronica Violet

Sleep well,
wake warm,
bright shell;

sleep well
tell bell
till dawn;
sleep well,
wake warm.

TAUTOGRAM

Temporal

The twigs touching the water
trace tree tunes
that telegraph time's tensions,
taut transfigurations.

The Tautogram consists of verse in which all the words begin with
the same letter. The form was invented in the 1960s by members of
the OULIPO movement. OULIPO also invented variant forms of
the Sestina and Rhopalic verse.

REVERDIE

Spring

Under blossoms that tremble like water
daffodil trumpets, yellow as butter
fresh from the churn, are dancing like lovers
in swaying grass, in clarities of air.

Once brown meadows are slopes and scoops of green,
grass growing tall to please the lovers' need
to hide away from any that might see
their secret joys, their ecstasies of ease

triumphant, rapt in the great beginning,
the thrusting joy, the race that's run to win,
the leap of hope, the song that dancers sing
to clear blue sky high over sudden Spring.

The Reverdie is composed most usually of ten syllable lines, the
line endings being linked together by assonance or rhyme. It is a
poem celebrating spring and considered a dance poem. There are
usually five or six stanzas.

RIMAS DISSOLUTAS
_____

Completion

That tap upon the door is late,
and yet it would have been too soon
a very little while ago;
I hope he has not lost my name.

I have known what it means to wait
for destiny, have watched the moon
move every ocean to and fro,
lost in its pale reflected flame,

have played with words like death and fate,
have scryed the glass, have cast the rune,

have studied how the embers glow,
discarded weights of guilt and shame,

shed equally both love and hate,
have seen the darkness of high noon,
the white blaze of the night, although
both light and darkness are the same

when all is done, and mortal fate
means very little; I'm immune
at last to everything I know,
and it is high time that he came.

Rimas Dissolutas is the term for a stanzaic poem in which the
second and succeeding stanzas rhyme line by line with the first
stanza, but have no internal rhyme. The lines may be of any length
and there is no rule as to metre. The rhyme scheme of a poem in
quatrains may be summarized as A B C D * A B C D and so on.

RIME COUEE

Ignorance

There is so much I do not know
I wonder at myself, although
I'd not know more.
Leaves have no notion how they grow
and flames cannot caress the snow;
tides touch the shore

but can't begin to comprehend
the inland deserts; larks ascend

in soaring praise
of something, sure, but to one end?
How does a friend become a friend?
All things amaze

the mind that knows it cannot find
within itself that greater mind
omniscient, wise,
and logical, that humankind
believes its deity designed
as life's grand prize

although at death the all we've known
will shatter on the cold tombstone
or change into
shapes that no living thing may own,
but perhaps then I may be shown
what truths are true.

Rime Couee consists of a six line stanza with the rhyme scheme A
A B A A B, the A lines being longer than the B ones. No particular
metre or line length is prescribed.

RIME RICHE
_____

Speaking of Grass

A man can drink from the river. Yet the river flows.
—Patrick Lane

On the bank of the river,
the smooth-running narrow river,
seated upon the grass

I'm reminded "All flesh is grass".

We flourish, then wither and die
like grass, I suppose, but we die
only partly, leaving our roots
tangled and knotted like roots.

Was that what he wanted to say?
If he did, I can't gainsay
his metaphor at all,
for all the roots of us all

once we have died will sleep
a while then rise from sleep
and pierce the earth, new born.
Each Spring the grass is born

again from its roots, but is
it the same grass? If it is,
and quite unchanged, do we
not alter, and do we

have not one hope of change?
I think, like grass, we change,
maybe as slow as grass;
oats, barley, wheat were grass

far back in time. In time
we may learn how to learn.

Rime Riche occurs when two rhyming words are identical in their
consonant-vowel-consonant combination, as in Reign/rain. The
words may be, in fact, the same word carrying two different meanings or functions, as when a word appears first as a noun and then
as a verb (plan/plan) or with two possible meanings (fine = payment, fine = very good). A still further variety of Rime Riche is one

in which the word is repeated without any alteration of function or meaning. This last variety is rare.

TRIOLET

The Suggestion

We're not in love, at least not quite,
but can't we both pretend to be?
Let us not even think tonight
we're not in love, at least not quite,
for, darling, making love well might
change everything for you and me.
We're not in love, at least not quite,
but can't we both pretend to be?

The Triolet is an eight line poem in any metre and with any line length that has the first line repeated as the fourth and seventh line and the second line repeated as the last line. It could be given as A B A A b A B.

VILLANELLE

The Pursuit

There is a bright-haired woman following me;
I sense her presence everywhere I go;
some day I'll understand the mystery.

Dreams chill my sleep and I sleep fitfully,
but dawn brings radiance and once more I know
there is a bright-haired woman following me.

Her presence haunts me, but I may not see
through frosted panes more that she cares to show;
some day I'll understand the mystery,

will perhaps discover what must come to be.
My dreams are drifting like the drifting snow;
there is a bright-haired woman following me,

saddened, it seems by my humanity
that, locked in winter, knows no way to grow;
some day I'll understand the mystery,

stand face to face with her and she with me
and ice will crack and history's rivers flow;
there is a bright-haired woman following me;
some day I'll understand the mystery.

The Villanelle consists of five stanzas of three lines and one of
four. The rhyme scheme is A B A, A B A, A B A , A B A, A B A , A B A A.
The first and third lines of the poem form the last lines of the four
subsequent stanzas in alternation, the first line of all being the first
to be repeated. The last stanza ends with the first and third lines of
the poem as a rhymed couplet.

Song for Beltaine II

On this holiday
customs have their say
and bring
children out to play
in their heart-whole way
and sing
rhymes and songs, display
gladness at this day
of Spring.

Dancers have their fling;
round the pole they swing
and sway,
making a great ring,
young folk promising
to stay
flirting, carolling,
courting, revelling
all May.

The Virelai is composed in stanzas of nine lines, some of five syllables and some of two. The long lines rhyme with each other as do the short ones, but the rhyme endings of the shorter lines in one stanza become the rhyme endings of the longer lines in the stanza following.

Syllables: 5 5 2 5 5 2 5 5 2
Rhymes: A A B A A B A A B

The final stanza of the poem has its shorter lines using the same rhyme sounds as the longer lines of the first stanza.

G E R M A N

Sleight Of Hand

Upon the table my hand, palm down, is still,
wholly removed from my own mind and will.

I watch it as I would watch an unknown beast
slithered up on shore from the sea to rest.

It is ignoring me; fingers widely-spread,
it seems to be staring patiently ahead.

Was I wrong to believe it wholly blind?
It must have some way to recognize its own kind,

I suddenly suppose. Now the fingers stir.
It is almost as if some strange presence in the air

has made itself felt. It humps itself. It seems
as if it is clutching something. Perhaps it dreams.

Can a hand really hallucinate or think?
Watching, I wonder if I've not reached the brink

of reason, pondering in this way my own hand.
And yet it moves as if something significant's planned,

and painfully swiveling round upon my wrist
has bent the fingers down to make a fist

that I am sure is concealing some object that
it has discovered, though god knows why or what

and where it came from. I watch, stupefied.
I can't believe my hand has a thing to hide.

But the fingers unfold on emptiness and it's clear
nothing is nearer than far, or farther than near.

The Knittelvers consists of a set of rhyming couplets, each line
having four stressed syllables and a variable number of unstressed
ones. After the fifteenth century, the lines were regularly of nine
syllables.

NIBELUNGEN STANZA

Wood in August

For Herbert Siebner

Alone between the warm trees
    I hear the branches stir
and think of gusting Spring gales,
    but nothing moves the air;
all breath is still; the far sky
    is cloudless, blue and clear;
the only sound is tree-sound,
    the slide of time, the growing year.

The shifts of time, the years' moves
    we never understand

until, alone between trees,
   a warmth on either hand,
we share the way our earth moves,
   our moons and tidals climb,
and, hidden deep in bone, find
   the surging years, the slide of time.

The Nibelungen Stanza is composed of two couplets, each of which is made up of two half lines or hemistiches.

Metre: ⏑′ ⏑′ ⏑′′ : ⏑′ ⏑′ ⏑′ (or ⏑′⏑)
     ⏑′ ⏑′ ⏑′′ : ⏑′ ⏑′ ⏑′ (or ⏑′⏑)
     ⏑′ ⏑′ ⏑′′ : ⏑′ ⏑′ ⏑′ (or ⏑′⏑)
     ⏑′ ⏑′ ⏑′′ : ⏑′ ⏑′ ⏑′ ⏑′.

Rhyme scheme: A A B B

SCHUTTELREIM

Threesome

Springtime's triad — thrush, lark, dove,
tell the sunlight their dark love.

Schuttelreim is the term for a rhyming couplet in which the two end words exchange their initial consonants as in a spoonerism.

HEBREW

In the Art Museum

All the galleries'
Burdened walls
Call up the dead.

Death has fingered
Every image,
Finished each frame.

Great ones we call them,
Heroes and Masters,
Incoherently awed.

Joyous or grieving,
Kind, cruel, or savage,
Loving or loathing,

Memory reveres them
No less than the pantheon
Of gods on Olympus.

Passion possessed them,
Queried the spiritual
Role of the senses.

Subtly made sketches,
Tortuous canvases

Uncover human

Vision while etchings
Wake bitter darkness,
Xylographs challenge.

Young and old, these are
Zeal and compulsion.

The Abecedarius is an acrostic in which each line, or perhaps stanza, opens with a fresh letter of the alphabet. These are in sequence until the alphabet is completed. Because the earliest verses in this form are Semitic, I have used the short line common in Hebrew verse.

TRADITIONAL

At Delphi

Do not believe me;
do not trust me:
I am the tide
and the empty shore;
I am a footprint
on old smooth stone
and I am stone
when it has gone.

This traditional verse structure has been termed "Parallelismus Membrorum." It is characterised by lines having parallel constructions and presenting antitheses and complementary extensions. The lines are usually short, containing only three or four words.

H I N D I

Distrust

Sliding under the twisted grey twigs of the torn bush,
   the foot-long snake endangers no one, nothing,
yet, like a whisper in the night, disturbs complacence,
   telling us tales whose memories hiss and sting.

The Doha is a rhyming couplet, the lines being of 24 syllables divided into two parts of 13 and 11 syllables. I have arranged the couplet as a quatrain.

IRISH

Two in a Garden

Lovers, we lie wondering
why our amorous leisure's
marred by spectres blundering
through our pastoral pleasures

under trees' tranquillity,
blossoming boughs above us,
whispering futility
and names of other lovers.

The Ae Freslige may be summarised as follows: the numbers in the brackets indicating the number of syllables in the last word of the line:

Syllables: 7(3) 7(2) 7(3) 7(2)
End rhymes: A   B   A   B

Breccbairdne

Spring Sprung

Joyful and wanton
Spring is awakening:
green spears are quivering

and buds boldly Swelling.

Sharing its graceful
spread petals the golden
primrose is gleaming
all over the garden.

Birth is beginning;
the daffodils, bouncing
their clusters of belfries,
are pealing, rejoicing.

Birds are attempting
the rituals of nesting
with twigs and straw, tatters
and scraps they are testing.

Life is in riot,
roaring, unreasoning;
restless, irrational
I find myself writing

verses that wonder
what happens to winter,
then wonder why ever
they bother to wonder

for this is Springtime
and no time for questions
on serious subjects
but for the glad season's

singing and dancing,
for laughter and playful
games of the goddess,
wanton and joyful.

Breccbairdne:
    Syllables: 5(2) 6(2) 6(2) 6(2)
    End rhymes: A   B   C   B
    All the end words consonate.

CASBAIRDNE

The Wilderness

Mysteries are obstacles
to the strictly sensible,
wilderness ridiculous
and absurdly bountiful

all of it untidiness,
such useless territories
only good for infantile
fancies and effronteries,

but Earth's irresponsible,
shapes unstable histories,
and retains love's wilderness
as mankind its mysteries.

Casbairdne:
    Syllables: 7(3) 7(3) 7(3) 7(3)
    End rhymes: A   B   C   D
    The end words A and C are in consonance with the B word. The
final syllable of line 4 alliterates with the stressed syllable preceding it. The end words of lines 1 and 3 rhyme with words in the
middle of lines 2 and 4 respectively.

Observation

Oceans rise,
forests fall;
Time, watching,
sees it all.

Time, watching,
sees the rocks
break under
earthquake shocks,

sees rivers
dry to stone,
each creature
shrunk to bone,

roots withered
black as grain,
men, women
eating pain,

humankind
at an end.
Time, watching,
can't pretend

grief, shock; in
pale clear eyes
oceans fall,
forests rise.

Cethramtu Rannaigechta Moire:
    Syllables: 3(1) 3(1) 3(1) 3(1)
    End rhymes: A   B   C   B

CRO CUMAISC ETIR CASBAIRDNI OCUS LETHRANNAIGECHT

Time Past

Time is long forgetting
and a drifting mist
that softens our regretting,
veils the loves we've kissed,

and reshapes our emotions
so we are not hurt
by long ago devotions
that destroyed the heart.

Dismissing as delusions
shames our nights recall,
it simplifies confusions
but lets the curtain fall

on much we would remember
if we only could —
something about December,
something in a wood,

his name, her name, possessions
that are lost to view;
now even our confessions
can't be wholly true.

Time past is a condition
of our being here,
and if that means omission
of delight or fear,

it means, too, expectation
and new hills to climb
preserved from hesitation
by forgetful Time.

Cro Cumaisc Etir Casbairdni Ocus Lethrannaigecht:
　　Syllables:　　　7(3)　5(1)　7(3)　5(1)
　　End rhymes:　　A　　　B　　　A　　　B
　　The third line may sometimes end with a disyllabic word that
rhymes into the middle of the following line. This is called an "aicill"
rhyme.

Beehive Huts, West Kerry

For John Montague

Behind the farmyard the beehives,
grey stone dwellings
for dark tribes and their children
wildly tumbling

the green slopes edging the ocean
seem to huddle
in the mist as if they're hiding

tired of muddles

we have made, just as we've also
marred and hindered
worship in the sacred places
of past kindred

whose simplicities of wisdom
our days disdain,
calling these stone houses hovels,
yet they remain

reminders of how time changes
almost nothing
essential; we still are mortal,
fragile, living

however we can in countries
we've not designed,
dreaming we may, death-deceiving,
leave truths behind.

Dechnad Cummaisc:
    Syllables: 8(2) 4(2) 8(2) 4(2)
    End rhymes: A   B   C   B
    The last word of line 3 rhymes into the middle of line 4 (Aicill
rhyme), sometimes the syllabic pattern is 8 4 4 8.

The Wood at Evening

Walking the wood at day's end,
sensing in every sound
wandering words of the wind
hinting at futures to find,

I think of the way a woman
answers a glance with a glance,
scanning farther than reason,
teaching her music to man,

and touch a tree in wonder,
pondering ways that wisdom
comes from bewitching woman,
from winds in trees while walking.

Dechnad Mor:
    Syllables: 8(2) 6(2) 8(2) 6(2)
    End rhymes: A   B   A   B
    The rhymes are, in fact, consonance. The first two lines rhyme
with each other in the body of the lines, as do the second two lines.
In the first two lines the rhyme may be no more than consonance,
but in the second two, it must be true rhyme. The last word of the
third line rhymes with one in the middle of the fourth line. Each
line should contain two words that alliterate with each other.

Young

For Xan

Seeing you smile, I despair
ever of watching over
you in your long years ahead
for deadly Time's defeated

many more worthy than I
and I know none less likely
now to find favour with fate,
having no mite of merit.

Yet you yourself, if you wish
and care, could make me flourish;
imagine me young once more
and Time, turning hopes over,

will grant long life, for no one
could rule out a revision
from one so wise and so young,
seeing the smile I'm seeing.

Deibide:
    Syllables: 7 7 7 7
    End rhymes: A A B B

The first and third lines end with stressed syllables the second
and fourth lines with unstressed ones. The last word of the stanza
alliterates with the preceding stressed word. The last word of the
third line rhymes with a word in the middle of the line following.
The rhyming of a stressed with an unstressed syllable is referred to
as "Deibide" rhyme.

For A Newborn God-Daughter

Here, alone,
I think of the vast unknown
enclosed in your wrinkled kissed
fist

that, intent
upon heaven's now lost extent,
fumbles to find and to keep
sleep.

Deibide Baise Fri Toin:
   Syllables: 3(2) 7(2) 7(1) 1(1)
   End rhymes: A   A   B   B

DEIBIDE GUILBNECH

By the Lake

Beyond the quivering reeds
a flicker of brightness leads
the watcher upon the shore
to repudiate earth-lore,

become a breath on the lake,
a ripple, a drifting flake,
a speck, a reflected white
wool cloud, wet-bright as the light,

not man at all, but a part
of the water's beating heart
and Time's beginning, in bond
to this one dawn and beyond.

Deibide Guilbnech:
    Syllables: 7(1) 7(1) 7(1) 7(1)
    End rhymes: A   A   B   B
    In this variation of the Deibide formula all the endrhymes are
stressed. There is alliteration and internal rhyme as in Deibide.

DEIBIDE GUILBNECH DIALTACH

The Visitant

For Brigid

Arms raised to praise the earth
for stirrings of coming birth
I find I am holding my breath
in case I should embrace death.

But I am feeling the leap
and kick of a soul from sleep,
the lunge and twitch of a shape
about to achieve escape

with a vital delightful zest
that time will put to the test
from the naked squalling start,
and now, here, under her heart

I know there are joys and tears,
miracles, wonders, fears,
a future of storms and calms,
mankind new-born in her arms.

Deibide Guilbnech Dialtach:
    Syllables: 7(1) 7(1) 7(1) 7(1)
    End rhymes: A   A   B   B
    All the end words consonate.

Droigneach

Samhain

For Alison

Mystery attends the year when Earth confesses
an uncontrollable need of celebration
and each leaf in the Autumn orchard expresses
in ochre and bronze and crimson the conflagration

needed now the seasons are nearing transition,
the fire that is power and pride and supervenes
whenever the slowing sun threatens inanition,
pallid and shadowy over the evergreens

that still spire upwards, needles gaunt, unchanging,
remote, it would seem, from the earth's predicament.
There comes a time in the year when, rearranging
summer memories, colours rustling, resplendent,

the crisp dry leaves call out to us and, responding,
we build a fire of the broken and dismembered
fragments of earthly suffering and, extending
hands to the dead who are, in this blaze, remembered,

celebrate the riches we've known, the profusion,
the births, the dearths, the ever changing history,
finding in fire a vision beyond illusion,
welcoming the holiness and the mystery.

Droighneach:
    Syllables: 9-13(3) 9-13(3) 9-13(3) 9-13(3)
    End rhymes: A   B   A   B
    A stanza may be composed of several quatrains if so desired.

LETHRANNAEGECHT MOR
_____

Connemara

For Susan Musgrave

Connemara, green
blest country of stone
where the sea-mists shine
a light all their own,

I am with you still;
though a long time stray
you must feel me stand
where the dolmens pray

in their rain-soft veils

to the wise ones above
the huddled thatched roofs,
the round hills we love,

the silver white strands,
the mounds of brown weed,
the tides lapping land
for all of us need

to stand where we can
and speak to those gone
beyond the soft green
and the grey scattered stone.

Lethrannaigecht Mor:
    Syllables: 5(1) 5(1) 5(1) 5(1)
    End rhymes: A   B   C   B
    If the last word of the third line does not rhyme into the middle
of the fourth line, then the A and C words should consonate with
the B word. This is an early rule. Later the consonantal linking was
replaced by aicill rhyme. The first two lines are linked by assonance within the lines. This device is called "amus."

RANNAIGECHT

Outcrop

Land under me, watching the stars,
I stroll the high field and stand
upon moss-covered granite,
the ancient grain of the land.

On bedrock here, I return
to the pulse of this old stone
under me, earth's origin
within the wind and the rain

abrading and changing all,
creating gravel and loam,
cutting the canyon's channel,
providing the runnels with room

hugely to deepen and swell
till, rivers, they meet the sea
that, moving to the moon-pulse,
evolved all the life to be.

Or so, here, under the stars
I tell myself as I stand
on the moss-covered granite,
the signature of the land.

Rannaigecht:
    Syllables: 7(1) 7(1) 7(2) 7(1)
    End rhymes: A   B   C   B
    There is aicill rhyme in lines 3 and 4 and sometimes in lines 1
and 2. The final words of lines 1, 2 and 4 consonate.

The Making of Music

Piping men thought that music
was taken from a feather
of sly Eros by magic
to trick and tease the hearer

with sounds for dancing lovers,
enlivening the passions,
contriving sentimental
lies to spur seductions.

I'm not of this opinion,
preferring to consider
our music wholly sea-born,
the moon our one composer,

except, of course, for certain
tuneful fantasies stepping
lightly around our garden,
for there I hear Pan piping.

Rannaigecht Bec I:
    Syllables: 7(2) 7(2) 7(2) 7(2)
    End rhymes: A   B   A   B
    The rhyming is, in fact, consonance rather than true rhyme.
Line 3 has an aicill rhyme with line 4 and the final word of line 4
alliterates with the word immediately preceding it.

Against Learning

No learning
can answer the tides turning
under the moon or reply
to the cry of the sun burning,

or ever
understand any lover
trapped in the pains of pleasure,
all mind-made measures over,

for passion
is one with the tides' action,
the sun's heat, the moon's control;
thus all souls, in their fashion

wise, discerning,
praise scholarship for its turning
to vision and to insight,
sunlit and moonlit learning.

Rannaigecht Bec II:
    Syllables: 3(2) 7(2) 7(2) 7(2)
    End rhymes: A   A   B   A
    The final word of the third line has an aicill rhyme with the middle of the fourth. There is a variant form in which we find: End rhymes A B A B. The end words of lines three and four may alliterate. This is a shortened form that has been called Rannaigecht Chetharchubaid Gairit Recomarcach.

The Names

Air me your favorite name,
one you would give to a stone
you felt had a pulse of flame
untamed by the known, alone

there on the earth at your feet,
or tell me the name you'd give
to the first child that you meet
in the street where lovers live,

or the one you long to write
on vellum to see it shine
with elegance and delight,
bright as the sacred sign

on gospels in bishops' courts,
or tell me the name you share
with nothing in human thoughts,
but with water, earth, fire, air.

Rannaigecht Mor:
    Syllables: 7(1) 7(1) 7(1) 7(1)
    End rhymes: A   B   A   B
    The rhyming is, in fact, consonance. The final word of line 3
has an aicill rhyme with the middle of line 4 and the last word of
line 4 alliterates with the preceding word.

Crepuscule

For Sylvia

Nearing night
as day is a dying light
and we walk our island home
the ripples of foam are bright.

Twilight brings
that brightness to many things,
suffusing the hours we spend
as we end our wanderings

blessed by white
walled rooms where today I write
of loving and living here
contentedly nearing night.

Rannaigecht Mor Gairit:
    Syllables: 3(1) 7(1) 7(1) 7(1)
    End rhymes: A   A   B   A
    The last word of the third line has an aicill rhyme into the middle of the line following.

R o w a n

For Lawrence Maynard

Reason can not explain
how the Autumn rowan
history thought holy
found its vivid crimson.

Legends have their answers,
Christian and Pagan;
they are only stories
setting out a pattern

suitable for children
playing in the garden.
I find myself driven
to an older version,

feel those berries risen
from a burning brightness
in the heart of silence
where I see the Goddess

standing like a rowan
crowned by more than crimson,
giving man a present
of her own heart's reason.

Rinnard:
   Syllables: 6(2) 6(2) 6(2) 6(2)
   End rhymes: A   B   C   B

The A and c words consonate with B. There is an aicill rhyme between lines 3 and 4.

Alba

Leaving her still sleeping
underneath the covers
safe from winter's cramping
is usual for lovers

who discover pleasure
in precluding grieving
and a kind of grandeur
in a well-planned leaving.

Rionnaird Tri-Nard:
    Syllables: 6(2) 6(2) 6(2) 6(2)
    End rhymes: A   B   C   B
    Line 3 consonates with lines 2 and 4. The last syllable of the first line alliterates with the first stressed syllable of the second. The last words of lines 2 and 3 rhyme into the middle of lines 3 and 4 respectively.

Intermission

Gone to lie in leaf-lit dapple,
drowsing in the summer sun,
sky is simply a blue bubble,
mind a mummer babbling on.

Crows caw no concern or worry;
wildfowl float serenely by;
nothing here's prepared to hurry;
no one needs to probe or pry.

Even bees seize the occasion,
crawling slowly round warm blooms,
revelling in languid leisure;
spiders cease to work their looms.

Yet the fretful world is waiting
worriedly to hurry on
and Fall's bell will soon be sounding,
summer pleasure spurned and gone.

Seadna:
    Syllables: 8(2) 7(1) 8(2) 7(1)
    End rhymes: A   B   C   B
    The last word of the first line alliterates with the first stressed
word of the line following. The third line rhymes with the stressed
word immediately preceding the last word of the stanza, and the
last word of the stanza alliterates with both these words.

Pike

For Diane Keating

Reasoning beside the river
bridge, I sense his position,
an old one ageless in wisdom,
wanton with erudition,

lurking as knowledge is lurking
always, lost and forgotten,
crippled by history's burden,
great books burned or forbidden.

Learning is always relearning;
loss is always happening;
a pike haunts every river,
hiding from our reasoning.

Seadna Mor:
    Syllables: 8(2) 7(3) 8(2) 7(3)
    End rhymes: A   B   C   B
    Apart from the altered organization of the syllables, Seadna Mor
is identical with Seadna.

The Old Ones

Darkness wears
chains of stars
and bestows
mysteries;
star-blest there
wise ones bear
spells to share
sorceries.

Words enfold
chains of gold,
glittering old
fineries,
with a spell
wish earth well,
say "Farewell
miseries!"

Strong of heart,
they take part
in all art's
masteries,
old in soul
shape the bowl
that heals whole
histories.

Snam Suad:
  Syllables: 3(1) 3(1) 3(1) 3(3) 3(1) 3(1) 3(1) 3(3)
  End rhymes: A   A   B   C   D   D   D   C

The A rhymes may be imperfect. Lines 2 and 3 are linked by consonance. The lines 3 and 4, 6 and 7, 4 and 7 are linked by alliteration. The seventh line contains alliteration.

SNED-BAIRDNE

Orchard Incident

Shaking the tatter-leaved branches
in the garden
to bring down the withered apples,
scarred and hardened

by weathers of wet wild autumn,
and then stooping
to tangled grass where they've hidden,
grasping, groping,

gathering this last hurt harvest,
I'm unmaking
apple dreams, their night's daybreaker
waking, shaking.

Sned-Bairdne:
    Syllables: 8(2) 4(2) 8(2) 4(2)
    End rhymes: A   B   C   B
    In line 4 every stressed word must rhyme. The A and C end words consonate with the B word.

The Toys

Day ended,
I look back and remember
the toys nobody mended.

Wheels shattered,
heads cracked, lead men dismembered,
parts lost, none of it mattered.

My grieving
was childish and natural,
but quite soon I'd be leaving

home for all
those boarding school solitudes,
the massed prayers, the football,

and learning
myself, my own sensations;
there could be no returning

though haunted
sometimes by sad disturbing
thoughts of toys that I'd wanted

to possess
always, loyal, devoted,
for they were the happiness,

the sorrow,
the friends and companions

of each day, each tomorrow.

Day ended,
I look back and remember
the toys nobody mended.

Treochair:
    Syllables: 3(2) 7(3) 7(2)
    End rhymes: A   B   A
    There is frequent alliteration.

TRIAN RANNAIGECHTA MOIRE

On the Moor

For Jane Urquhart

A lone pleasure's
wandering where
purple heather,
haunting air,

appears to move
within the eye
as if a mode
of memory,

a kind of dream
that is a past
we never knew
and never lost

but keep within
the marrow bone
and feel it when
we walk alone.

Trian Rannaigechta Moire:
  Syllables: 4(1) 4(1) 4(1) 4(1)
  End rhymes: A   B   C   B
All the end words of the lines consonate. There is aicill rhyme
between the third and fourth lines.

UNNAMED METRE (MURPHY 8)

The Well

I at wellhead,
leaning over,
   see wet gold;
it shines, shaking
in the water;
   I've been told

there is magic
in this vision
   of the sun;
trembling, spinning
in the darkness,
   it means one

could find fortune
here by wishing
   the right way,
gain a treasure
or a lover.
   Some folk say

this is rubbish,
but some others
   won't deny
the old story;
seeking glory,
   nor will I.

Unnamed metre (Murphy 8):
  Syllables: 4(2) 4(2) 3(1) 4(2) 4(2) 3(1)
  End rhymes: A   B   C   D   E   C

UNNAMED METRE (MURPHY 12)

At Knocknarea

In Memoriam Robert Speaight

Still beneath Knocknarea,
watching my friend climb
to the cairn, days fell away;
we escaped from Time,

no longer friends at all
but part of a dream

mankind knows perpetual
as willow and stream,

his tread inscribing the mound
with letters to say
"Man only finds the long found,
prays how ages pray.

Whether or not you climb high
or remain below
you breathe in the distant sky,
grow as grasses grow,

but to some is there given,
and suddenly, light
breaking from earth or heaven."
Sharp etched on my sight,

smaller and smaller he grew.
Then he stood alone
beside great Maeve and I knew
he communed with stone

for an infinite moment.
Returned down the hill,
he took my hand; the current
sustained him still.

Unnamed Metre (Murphy 12):
   Syllables: 7 (1, 2 or 3) 5(1) 7(1, 2 or 3) 5(1)
   End rhymes: A   B   A   B
   The end word of line 3 rhymes into the middle of line 4 (aicill rhyme). The A rhymes are permitted to be approximate.

Playing the Game

Anyone rhymed it:
Give us a penny
(the game that summer)
I have not any.

Playtime is over
maybe for ever.
Now it is *Give me*
a new young lover,

knowing the answer
before it's spoken.
Dreaming is over,
the mirror broken,

one hope remaining,
last of the many;
Give me a reason.
I have not any.

Unnamed metre (Murphy 18):
    Syllables: 5(2) 5(2) 5(2) 5(2)
    End rhymes: A   B   A   B
    The B rhymes are constant, but the A rhymes may be either imperfect or omitted. Occasion aicill rhyme occurs between lines 1 and 4.

ITALIAN

In the Ninth Month

For Brigid

There is a heaviness in imminent birth,
a slowing of the shallow burdened breath,
a labouring of the limbs as if this birth,
compact in energy, were giving birth
foreknowledge of the clumsiness of youth
and the tense discomfort of rebirth
at puberty; while limbering up for birth
I wonder if there, too, are dreams of death,
of, maybe, a return by way of death
to some prenatal source whose timeless truth
now drifts away before our mortal truth.

Or is there space within the womb for truth
of any kind? The urgency is birth
and the encountering of a place where truth
is what small fingers find, and absolute truth
what hunger needs, while ventures of the breath
creating sound assert another truth,
demand obedience, formulating truth
from need as peoples, nations, in their youth
have done, still do. Need is the cry of youth
but that need is no nearer to the truth
than is the lunge of love to whimpering death,

though orgasm has been called 'the little death'.

But 'What is Truth?' asked Pilate, granting death
and thus to millions a burning truth.
Lost at birth and found again at death
it exists beyond both birth and death
they tell us, adding that the shock of birth
is a forgetting and a kind of death,
being the first step on the road to death
as well as a relinquishing of the breath
of timelessness to draw fresh mortal breath.
We're also told desire's a form of death
and that the glorious passions of our youth
are folly, as are all the needs of youth.

Yet is there not a touch of truth in youth,
even, perhaps, in its discounting death?
The sheer untamed vitality of youth
brings dreams and visions reaching beyond youth —
poems, paintings, compositions that give truth
a fresh perspective, showing age the youth

it has forgotten. Childhood and then youth
bring radiant astonishments to birth
and every human shouting out its birth
returns this old and battered earth to youth,
grants it the simple wonderment of breath
and of the *spiritus* men called the breath.

This child, curved now around the hours to birth,
entering upon our world of shifting breath,
reborn to childhood, then reborn to youth,
to womanhood or manhood, then to death
is life continual and the only truth.

There are no rules establishing the number of syllables in or the metre of the lines of the Canzone. There are no end rhymes as such. The end words of the first of five, twelve line stanzas are repeated in the following four stanzas, and then in a four-line envoi. The established word order is as follows:

ABAACAADDAEE * EAEEBEECCEDD * DEDDADDBBDCC *
CDCCECCAACBB * BCBBDBBEEBAA * ABCDE

There are only five end words in this form of the Canzone. Other patterns have also been used, but this is the most generally accepted formula.

DECIMA ITALIANIA
_____

Samhain In Perugia II

Somewhere beyond the broken wall
a shudder in the moonlit grass
responding to a long dead call
lets century upon century pass
unchallenged through the gates of time.
I, leaning on my window ledge,
half see, half hear the shadows throng
all eased of every vow and pledge,
the flags, the banners, and the long
and thunderous guns, the sweat, the grime.

Etruscans, Romans, Goths, Guelphs, all
of these and more crowd in the town;
one would expect them to recall
deeds their historians have set down,
but this is not why they are here.
They have returned to feel once more
the touch of skin, the nudge of bone,

to be the way they were before
the one unknown thing became known
and they lost all desire and fear.

Now they, this one night, feel again
the ignorance, the needless guilt,
the innocence of love and pain,
and, where their kindred's blood was spilt,
the sorrow they were born to need.
I watch them move slow shadows through
the narrow steep streets and the squares,
climb stairs, mount walls; all that they knew
is ours, and all we feel is theirs
this night for them to touch and heed.

Dawn slides up its November sun;
roofs walls and towers reclaim their day
and all the multitudes have gone,
though here and there stray memories stay
like wisps or threads snagged on a stone.
I leave my window, turn to sleep
too tired to think or question where
they may have gone and what they'll keep
of all they found, and if they'll bear
again somewhere this flesh, this bone.

The Decima Italiana is a stanza form composed of ten, eight syllable lines with the rhyme scheme A B A B C * D E D E C. The c words must be stressed and the first D line must begin a new sentence.

In Passing

I glimpsed it from the corner of my eye,
a sudden flicker in the bevelled pane
of our front door. Could it be her again,
the little ghost that used to wander by
the garden bushes and then vanish, shy
perhaps or perhaps afraid? Like drifting rain
she moved along the grass, as clear and plain
in this shared universe as you or I.

The Italian Octave consists of eight lines of iambic pentameter
with the rhyme scheme A B B A A B B A.

Milan Cathedral

for Peter Schwartz

The marble figures poised above the square
remote from city grime and fume and sweat
restate the edge of time, a parapet
we leap from, trusting paradise to prayer.

The Italian Quatrain consists of four lines of iambic pentameter
rhyming A B B A. It differs from the In Memoriam stanza only in
its length.

Her

I know that she had long black hair
and maybe even has it still,
but have not ever known her name;
I've held her clothed, I've held her bare
and we have shared the ultimate thrill;
our pride has scorched us like a flame.

And yet, though all of this is true
were she dismissed as fantasy
the label would not be a lie,
for it was she who brought me to
the edge of time where I could see
creation's moment rolling by.

The Italian Sestet is a six line stanza of octosyllabic lines rhyming
A B C A B C.

OTTAVA RIMA

Perugian Nocturne

The town is evening's. Dawn shuffles by
without disturbing anyone but those
who raise their shutters to the wakening sky,
while high noon is a shadowless repose,

a closure of the mind, a dusty sigh
to sleeping pigeons, but then shadow grows
and slowly spreads its edges to define
the shape of things, establish their design.

Now we can walk securely, hear and see
the sharp precisions of the street and square:
the lucent windows offer luxury
and there's a crispness coming on the air,
a breathless taste of clarities to be
as in the restaurant shining cooks prepare
the appetite and summary of the day
a stage set for the actors in the play

that now begins its poised penultimate act
as young and old, wives, mothers, fathers meet
in promenade, determined to exact
each ounce of pleasure from the teeming street,
toddlers in harness, women bloused and slacked,
men arguing with customary heat,
as shadows deepen into gentle night,
and street lamps spread their comfortable light.

Soon it will end and people drift away,
but here, this evening, now, all is at one;
the medieval walls exhale the day
and breathe at ease, unfettered by the sun;
kindred recover kindred, children play,
and lovers find each other; day is done,
dark not yet here; this is the time between
when what we see is what the gods have seen.

Ottava Rima is composed of eight iambic pentameter lines with
the rhyme scheme A B A B A B C C.

First Words

We're told "In the beginning was the Word",
but was it in a language we might hear
or in another that evades the ear
to speak in silences? It seems absurd
but, standing by the ocean, once I heard
not speech exactly but a cadence clear
as actual sound as if I had come near
to learning how all syllables occurred.

I think it our first language still unknown
to grammar, never measured into sound;
the message is itself the messenger
who reaches us when without thought, alone,
we seek for nothing and know we have found
the very breathless centre of the air.

The Petrarchan Sonnet consists of 14 iambic lines of ten syllables
with a break after the eighth line, and the rhyme scheme A B B A A
B B A * C D E C D E.

The Voice

The half-heard voice that murmurs in the wood,
poised just behind me, close enough for breath
to brush my nape and agitate the blood

is not a threatening visitant from death

as other people have supposed and fled.
This is no spirit of the speechless dead
but of a dawn two night-long lovers stood
here, parting, and left whispers in the wood.

Commonly, the Rispetto has eight syllables in each line, but sometimes ten. The poem is composed of two quatrains, with the rhyme scheme running either A B A B * C C D D as here, or A B A B * C D C D.

The Lake

For Sylvia

The shining mirror of the lake
between dark mountain walls of fir
seems in a sleep no sound could wake,
no single sliding ripple stir,

lost in a peace man's never known
for all the journeys he has made;
I stand here troubled, half afraid,
and bend my back and throw a stone.

The Rispetto usually has eight syllables in each line, but there may be ten. It is composed of two quatrains with the rhyme scheme A B A B * C D D C as here, or C D C D, or C C D D.

Peace

Every day a dream of peace
disturbs us, will not let us rest
who cannot give ourselves the calm
of mind, the comfort and the ease
that cool the fevered skin and quiet
the raging heart till it is gentle.

We think that people should be gentle,
live in amity and peace,
never interrupt the quiet
security of a world at rest,
salve the wounded and bring ease
to troubles, grant the heartache calm.

We place our trust in words to calm
the furies, cure the tempests, gentle
passions, offer suffering ease;
we try to think there may be peace
somewhere for us, a place of rest
radiant in meditative quiet.

No matter what we say, the quiet
never lasts. The longed for calm
proves a storm centre and we rest
exhausted, far from any gentle
comfort with no hope of peace,
deprived of every shred of ease.

However much we long to ease
despair and pain and try to quiet

anguish, shaping words of peace,
there is no way that we can calm
earth's raging energies, make gentle
this world of change that will not rest.

There is no likelihood of rest
in this life emptied of all ease
where even death is rarely gentle.
The sounds of war are never quiet,
each pause in fury and each calm
a transient, fragmentary peace.

Will we rest ever in a quiet
place of ease and find the calm
that makes hearts gentle and at peace?

The Sestina is composed of six, six-line stanzas followed by a
three-line stanza. Usually, the Sestina is unrhymed. However, the
end words of the first stanza are repeated in each of the following
five stanzas in a set order; they are then placed in the last stanza
in the middle or at the end of the lines. The end word order is as
follows: ABCDEF FAEBDC CFDABE ECBFAD DEACFB BDFECA.
In the envoi the end words are E C A and the words in the middle
of the lines B D F.

R H Y M E D   S E S T I N A

Night Blossom in April

For Kathleen Raine

The flowering cherry tree,
a spectre in the night,

almost bewitches me;
trapped in the cool moonlight,
no show of snow could be
more frighteningly white.

Massed petals are so white
the brown boughs of the tree
have shed their shapes to be
one with surrounding night,
made humble by this light
that pales and troubles me.

The moon stares down on me
as if her mask of white
enchantment could send light
to blind me like this tree
that shudders to the night;
I fear that I might be

changed beyond change, could be
denatured. Dazzling me
in this moon-burdened night,
the blossoms' piercing white
irradiance clasps the tree
with more than natural light

for this is not the light
that shines to bless and be
the life of things. The tree
whose ghost-fire faces me
is more than a mere white
astonishment in the night,

for it has renamed night,
has redefined the light,
made black more black and white

more white than white can be;
its presence urges me
to burn bright as the tree

and every night to be
robed by the light in me
as white as this white tree.

Rhymed Sestinas in English were composed initially by Swinburne
and Clinton Scollard, though casual rhyme often appears in basically unrhymed Sestinas. There are no rules as to the metre or the
number of syllables in the line.

SICILIAN OCTAVE

At the End of the Day

The workmen underneath the house are done,
a curious quiet filters everywhere
as if the carpenters have not merely gone,
leaving their dusts to settle in the air,
their sawing and their hammering lingering on
like phantom echoes; something else is there,
a creature whose dark life has just begun
and one whose destinies we now must share.

The Sicilian Octave consists of eight lines of iambic pentameter
with the rhyme scheme A B A B A B A B.

Love in an English Garden

Our love will last the summer out;
just as this garden will endure
the sun, the wind, the rain without
uncertainties, we may be sure
our love will last the summer out.

Within the shadows of the trees
we, Berkeley-like, compose our day;
without us butterflies and bees
would be no more than shapes that play
within the shadows of the trees.

Why bother what the world's about,
that alien world our love has banned,
the world of riot, wrath, and rout?
As my hand reaches to your hand,
why bother what the world's about?

No hours are as calm as these
of summer and the roses' pride,
their silken petals speaking ease;
however many men have died,
no hours are as calm as these,

no loves less modified by doubt,
for we have altered earth and air,
renewed the fire, the sea, devout
in reverence for the gods, and swear
no love's less modified by doubt.

Our love will last the summer out
within the shadows of the trees.
Why bother what the world's about?
No hours are as calm as these,
no loves less modified by doubt.

The Sicilian Quintet is composed in iambic pentameter or tetrameter (as here). There are five lines in each stanza and each stanza ends with a repetition of its first line thus: A B A B A. There are six stanzas and the sixth one is composed of the repeated first lines of all the stanzas with the rhyme scheme A B A B A; consequently, the first lines of the first third and fifth stanzas must rhyme with each other, as must the first lines of the second and fourth stanzas.

SICILIAN SEPTET

That Dream Again

Last night I dreamed that narrow city lane
and met the brown cloaked woman in the hood,
the cobbles underfoot black-wet with rain.
I had dreamed her before and we had stood
like this, together. What could be more plain?
Remembrance lives like darkness in the blood;
no history vanishes without a stain.

The Sicilian Septet is composed of seven lines of ten syllables each, with the rhyme scheme A B A B A B A. The metre is iambic pentameter, ˇ ′ ˇ ′ ˇ ′ ˇ ′ ˇ ′.

The Excavation

When we were boys we dug a cavern here
under the orchard, busy-pawed as moles,
crouched in the dark without a doubt or fear,
passing earth back in tins and cast out bowls;
that cavern brought a secret glory near,
a golden gleam that bathed our boyhood souls,

a radiance that our dust-dried mouths could taste
as clearly as the flat warm lemonade
we passed from hand to hand as we embraced
a power older than the rule-book laid
upon us; at day's end, glad, cramped, we placed
turf, branches, leaves to hide the mine we'd made.

Of course we were discovered and were blamed
for "dangerous stupidity", were whipped
inevitably, (dreamers must be tamed),
then made to watch as lumbering fellows tipped
tins, refuse in that sacred place; ashamed —
for them not of ourselves — and sullen lipped,

we felt our vision scorned, our pride betrayed,
our freedom shackled and our needs unheard;
although we knew that urgent game we'd played
could be considered dangerous and absurd
we also knew, blessed by that escapade,
a dark and chthonic knowledge had been shared.

In the Sicilian Sestet each stanza, or poem, is composed of six lines of ten syllables each. The rhyme scheme is A B A B A B or, if termed an "Italian Sestet," A B C A B C. The metre is iambic pentameter, ‿ ′ ‿ ′ ‿ ′ ‿ ′ ‿ ′.

Gentle Ghost

She drifts along the corridor at night,
too dark, too subtle, to be clearly seen,
an undemanding ghost, petite and slight.
We can't be sure but think she may have been
a serving girl — quite certainly not white
but Chinese or Eurasian, seventeen
or thereabouts. We wonder if it's right
to let her walk this once familiar scene.

Perhaps she doesn't know she's gone astray
and should be somewhere else. It might be kind
to end her bondage, send her on her way
to that immensity her death designed.
Or does she walk untroubled by the way
we offer phantoms to her questing mind?

The Sicilian Sonnet consists of 14 lines of 10 syllables each. The rhyme scheme is A B A B A B A B * C D C D C D. The metre is iambic pentameter. This variant combines two Sicilian quatrains on one rhyme with a Sicilian sestet.

Dichotomy

Upon the path the cupped rose petals fall
in celebration of the living light
as climbing ivy eats away the wall.

A Sicilian Tercet consists of three lines of iambic pentameter rhyming A B A.

Shape Changers

In these shallows the pebbles I kneel to see,
transfiguring sunlight, rippling restlessly,
in altering their shapes are altering me.

The Stornello consists of three, eleven syllable lines end rhyming with one another, the second rhyming word being a near rhyme.

Another type of Stornello begins with a line of ten or fewer syllables, but then is composed in hendecayllables as here.

The omission of the words "kneel to" in the above would result in the making of the second type.

Timing

For Charles Lillard

Spring has returned once more, but its not the same
Spring that sent me prospecting when I was young;
it may be that aging embers cannot flame
and greed no longer tease with a cheating tongue,
boastful, persuasive, having no sense of shame —
or could it be that Time has finally hung
my hat up, scrubbed my licence, destroyed my claim,
driven me back from hope, my fiddle unstrung?

The Strambotto is a one stanza poem of eight, eleven syllable lines, with the rhyme scheme A B A B A B A B.

There are various forms of the Strambotto. Another form is composed of six lines rhyming, usually, A B A B A B. Other rhyme schemes also occur.

Corracha Cagalt

For Margaret Blackwood

The leaps and flickerings of flame
inside the black bars of the grate
are visitants we fear to name.

Some say that they foretell our fate,
hint everything that will befall,
inside the black bars of the grate.

The flames cast shadows on the wall;
dark shifting shapes that sway and swerve
hint everything that will befall,

flick dancing visions at the nerve.
As evening spreads across the earth
dark shifting shapes that sway and swerve

spell every phase of death and birth,
creations beyond earth's control;
as evening spreads across the earth

and we attempt to see life whole
the leaps and flickerings of flame,
creations beyond earth's control,
are visitants we fear to name.

The number of syllables in the Terzanelle is not regulated, but there are usually either eight or ten in each line. There are 19 lines.

Complete lines are repeated in this verse form. These are indicated with the symbol R attached to the capital letter indicating a repeated endword. Where there are two complete lines repeated and rhyming with each other, the second is numbered 2. AR1 BR AR2 * B CR BR * C DR CR * D ER DR * E FR ER * F AR1 F AR2. The final stanza could also be rhymed F FR AR1 AR2.

Verse on a Birthday

I do not know when I was born
although today I celebrate
the day on which my birth was known.

There is no way that I can date
my origin; I only know
both past and future lie in wait.

I am a gradual ceaseless flow
without beginning, without end,
a knowledge learning that I know

it is ridiculous to pretend
this shape you see, this name you trace,
are more than images I lend

the poverties of time and space;
mortality laid out the game
for which I donned this human face.

Each must be each and same be same
as we make moves through wrong and right,
so much involved that we maintain

there's nothing other and the flight
of time is actual and real,
while mass and energy unite

with mind to give us what we feel
to be ourselves, until we meet

that ruling that has no appeal

and, swaddled in our winding sheets,
are firmly told that we have died,
game over, done, for no heart beats,

no mind records, no love or pride
or sensibility remain.
Yet I refuse to be denied

my certainties and here maintain
that I am not of mortal kind;
I live and live and live again,
the servant of a life designed
as endless, travelling from the far
unto the far; my soul and mind

and mortal body merely are
devices proper to this place
dependent on a vivid star

that troubles us with time and space
until we sweep across the bar
to run another endless race.

Terza Rima is composed in three-line stanzas containing, usually, eight or ten syllables. The pattern of the end rhymes is A B A B C B C B C and so forth, ending with a couplet rhyming with the middle line of the last triplet or with a triplet whose first and third lines rhyme with the middle line of the preceding stanza, and whose middle line rhymes with the first and third lines of the preceding stanza, the two final stanzas thus forming the pattern A B A B A B. The metre is iambic: ᵕ ′ ᵕ ′ ᵕ ′ ᵕ ′ ᵕ ′.

Unanswerable

There is no way to answer anything;
faced with pebbles, broken leaves, or pale
shells upon the seashore glistening,

all our theories hesitate and fail.
There is no phrase of music and no word
with which we can reply; the run of quail

across the lawn, the ritual half absurd
half holy, puts all galleries to shame,
and there's no lyric anyone has heard

that can half touch the little dance of flame
there on the hearth. We need a keener skill
than any all our muses know to name,

one that we seek hopelessly until
we leave this life and learn what lives instill.

The Terza Rima Sonnet is composed of fourteen lines of iambic
pentameter with the rhyme scheme A B A B C B C D C D E D E E.

JAPANESE

CHOKA

The Tradition

For long centuries
poets wrote of love and parting.
Birds, trees, lakes, rivers
and the slant curtains of rain
made up their music.
For ageless generations
they created illusions
that became more real than real,
a true enchantment.
Must I say now tradition
is quite forgotten?
Rain trembles in cherry trees
and my daughters are singing.

The Choka alternates five with seven syllable lines, concluding with an additional seven syllable line. Thus a choka of nine lines would run: 5 7 5 7 5 7 5 7 7. The choka can be of any length, and is unrhymed and non-metrical.

In Passing

This cat the colour of smoke
slides out from the shrubbery
sinuous as the pleasures
of dreaming lovers.

The dodoitsu has four lines with the syllable count 7 7 7 5. It is unrhymed and non-metrical.

HAIKU

Conte

Gently on my cheek
the light kiss of my lover;
snowflakes in April.

The Haiku is composed of three unrhymed non-metrical lines with the syllable count 5 7 5. Haiku, traditionally, allude to the season of the year or to nature.

Nightwalker

Sleepless on warm summer nights
    I drift like a mist
through the narrows of the house,
    the alleys, the streets
crowded with all the people
    of my memories
busier than ever because
    of imminent dawn.

The Imayo is a poem of four, 12 syllable lines divided by a caesura after the seventh syllable, 7 * 5. I have indented the second part of each line in the above example. It is unrhymed and non-metrical.

I R O H A M O J I G U S A R I

The Trophy Room

Aghast at the furred heads, dumb,
choked, I say no word,
eager only to brush off
gory relics which,
inherited from the Raj,
keep place on your wall;
managing only a moan
of pain at your tales, I scrap
questionings that might appear
silly, for I can't

understand what mad motiv
wills you to tease and vex
your hearers with all this jazz.

The Iroha Mojigusari has the first letter of the alphabet opening the first line and the second letter of the alphabet concluding it. This continues until all the letters of the alphabet have been used in the correct order.

I have chosen to alternate 7 and 5 syllable lines as in the Choka, with one variation; because the verse has an odd number of lines, I have ended with a triplet rather than a couplet of seven syllable lines.

The spelling "motiv" is accepted in the larger dictionaries.

KATAUTA

Proposal

Will you sleep with me?
Your finger is in my glove
and I am wearing your shoes.

The Katauta is a three line, unrhymed and non-metrical poem with the syllable count 5 7 7. The first line poses a question and the following two lines answer it in a manner which, traditionally, appears to be spontaneous and intuitive.

Renewals

Winds in garden trees recall
forgotten freedoms;
in leaves old rain rephrases
questing centuries.

The Kouta (Little Song) has two forms. This one consists of four
lines with the syllable count of 7 5 7 5. The Kouta was a popular
song form of the Muromachi period.

In Age

I have almost forgiven
light for reshaping my face,
dark for not hiding the knowledge,
and time its whispers.

The second form of the Kouta (Little Song) consists of four lines
with the syllable count 7 7 7 5.

Tide Talk

Is death completion?
Breakers accomplish the shore.

The Mondo is an unrhymed and non-metrical poem of two lines. While there is no rule as to syllables, it would certainly approximate at least to the 5 7 syllabic count. The Mondo is formed of a one line question and a one line reply.

Are You There?

On telephone wires
each perched bird is a message
more lucid than wings.

Drop by drop from the slick eaves
rain is tapping out partings.

The words of the song
were lost on the leaf-strewn wind
as the shutters closed.

Mouth crammed with pebbles he tried
to out-distance the ocean.

When the black sail's brush

drew pain on the horizon
she bore a legend.

Tapping words out on the keys
I am echoing echoes.

The Renga alternates stanzas of 5 7 5 syllables with stanzas of 7 7.
It is unrhymed and non-metrical. The stanzas are linked by asso-
ciation, each echoing in some way an image or implication of its
predecessor. It is usually written by two (or more) poets in collabo-
ration.

SEDOKA

Under the Apple Tree

Light gently dances
over your thin cotton dress;
it is picking out flowers.

Above us the leaves
pass sunlight from hand to hand;
they are playing with water.

The Sedoka is composed of two stanzas each of 5 7 7 syllables. It is
unrhymed and non-metrical.

Not Really

I ambiguous?
No more than the way the reeds
write wind, write water.

The Senryu is an unrhymed non-metrical poem of three lines with
the syllable count 5 7 5.

Brief Encounter

Have you forgotten
that midnight on the beach,
the wavelets rippling
the pebbles as I proposed
and you turned, smiling, away?

How could I forget?
I was wearing my best dress
and salt stained the hem;
I do not know which of us
was the more ridiculous.

The Somonka consists of two stanzas with the syllable count 5 7 5
7 7. The first stanza is conventionally addressed by a lover to the
beloved, and the second stanza is the reply. It is unrhymed and
non-metrical.

Magical

A small statuette
of Her stands on my altar,
In the room corner
tremble tall peacock feathers.
On the page words are dancing.

The Waka consists of five lines with the syllable count 5 7 5 7 7.
The first two lines are each a complete sentence, as is the last line.
It is unrhymed and non-metrical.

JAVANESE

Nearing the End

Death comes close in the house around me,
    in the grey twilight of years murmuring
small sighed words to the floors, the ceilings
    and the walls' doorposts are tall prisoners;
each footstep in the evening echoes
    and the broad bedroom is awed, wondering
When? When? When? as the clock continues
    on its black spiked rounds without answering.

The Kakawin stanza consists of four lines of the same length in a chosen metre. The most popular metre for these stanzas, which were used for funeral rites quite frequently, was the Sardula-Vikridita metre which is made up of nineteen syllable lines with the following form: ′′′ ⌣⌣′ ′⌣′ ⌣⌣′ ′′⌣ ′′⌣ ⌣

I have chosen to break these lines after the ninth syllable.

On the Shore

Down on the shore the grey stone shingle stirs
to the reach of the tide;
gulls glide and swerve above us,
disregarding our affairs
and raucously shredding the air
as we watch how the water slides
its rhythmic death and rebirth;
everything under the sun
hears that perpetual chorus.

The lines have the following syllable counts, and the vowel sounds
of the last words in the lines are repeated in a pattern indicated
here as if they were rhymes, which they need not be:

    10A 6B 8C 7A 8A 8B 8A 8C 8C.

After the third decade of the sixteenth century, this verse form
was no longer used in Java but continued in Bali.

KASHMIRI

Thoughts at Evening

Shadows crossing twilit lakes
deepen the sad heart's darkness,
recalling songs long silenced,
loves lost, broken histories.

I can't recall face or name,
only a brightness, thin hands
touching leaves, an old garden,
rippling water, a scarred shrine,

yet brightness shines out still, held
in mind, in heart, as Truth's one
remnant, all else pared away
even sounds of silk sliding.

The Vakh consists of quatrains of seven syllable lines, each with
four stresses. It is occasionally rhymed or near-rhymed. This is a
fourteenth century form and was used by the woman poet Lalla-
Devi or Lal Ded.

K O R E A N

Night Dance

Dark as the night, her unloosed hair
descends and flows, changing her role;
no longer still, she moves, dances,
knowing the sounds, the sighs of wind
shaking the leaves, the white flowers.
Shall I tell you, shall I whisper
her married name? I will not tell.
Husbands are men; wives are women;
she only dances, though I believe
should she smile *yes*, her eyes shining,
dawn would delay, hold back until,
desire fulfilled, her fingers braid
dark as the night, her unloosed hair.

The Kasa consists of eight syllable lines. Each line is composed of
two phrases, or parts, of four syllables each.

There are no end rhymes, but there are headrhymes, each line
beginning with a syllable that rhymes or is in consonance with a
syllable at the beginning of another line.

In the Fall

In Memoriam Howard Millar

Carelessly leaves scatter down
   on the lawn that you have mown,
calling out in dry voices
   the syllables of a sly poem
captured from the wind that left
   your hands cold, your mind breathless.

The Sijo is composed of three lines, each of which is regarded as having several parts, their syllable count being 3 4 3 (or 4 4 * 3 4 3 (or 4) 4 * 3 5 4 3. Each line has a break after its first two groups of syllables. End rhyming does not occur. Head rhymes or initial consonance may occur, but neither are essential.

L A T I N

Autumn Evening

Staring through the window pane
   as the bare boughs shiver
I wonder why the bitter world
   has deprived earth's lover,
leaving emptiness and rain,
   nothing to discover
but damp earth and sodden leaves
   now the summer's over.

I turn back into the room
   where the firelight wanders
shadows round the darkling walls
   as the twilight wonders
where the night and whence the day
   and how the winter plunders
earth of all that colours bring,
   mourning Nature's blunders.

Yet there's a spirit giving
   winter's perseverance
strength to guard and to protect
   more than mere appearance,
animating these bare days
   with Time's old assurance
that enduring love's long need
   transforms endurance.

Goliardic verse is so termed because it was a popular verse form of the Goliards, the so-called Wandering Scholars of the twelfth and thirteenth centuries, who composed songs in rhymed and accented Latin verse. There are thirteen syllables in each line of the quatrain, and the line is divided after the seventh syllable. All four lines of the quatrain rhyme with each other and end on an unaccented syllable. In other words, the rhymes are feminine. Sometimes the last line of the quatrain has twelve syllables and is a hexameter. The most notable writer of Goliardic verse was the Archpoet who died in 1165 and whose *Confessio* is one of the great poems of the period.

LATVIAN

S u m m e r

Summer bends the distance, shaking
mountain slopes and climbing orchards,
dazing eyes with melting vision;
even air, transfigured, quivers.

The Daina is a quatrain with each line containing eight syllables.
There are no end rhymes though rhyme and alliteration may occur.
The metre is commonly trochaic; the lines all end on unstressed
syllables.

M A L A Y

After the Battle

The crows that crowd the broken trees
are black against a curdled sky;
what can we cull from histories
in which both light and reason die?

The Pantun which was modified and elaborated into the French
Pantoum in the nineteenth century is a quatrain rhyming A B A B,
and consists of two pairs of lines, the first making a statement which
proves to be a metaphor for the statement made in the second, or
which is the basis for an elaboration. There is internal consonance
and assonance.

MARATHI

Visak

The children on the cart,
their faces painted, shrilled
thin melodies that spilled
like bright water.

This was the birth and death
day of holy Buddha;
I noticed fronds shudder
on twilit palms

and in the kohl-rimmed eyes
of children saw a deep
darkness older than sleep
or night or mind,

a well from which arose
our universal dream
that seem is more than seem,
death less than death.

This metre is composed in lines of twenty-two syllables divided
into four parts, 6 6 6 and 4. The second and third parts rhyming.
These lines would be regarded in Western prosody as stanzas and I
have treated them as such.

S a m u n g l i

Outside my white-flaked muttee block
the land of ochre dust and rock
that watched the earthquake's hand unlock
eternities is silent.

No howl of dog or shite-hawk cry
disturbs the stiffness of the sky;
no dust-caked camels straggle by
the deserted village.

I kick a pebble. Nothingness
is now the spirit's one address,
its home from home where clocks express
neither past nor future.

This, the ultimate in between,
is where philosophy has been
discarded and religion seen
as wanton delusion,

and yet the mountain air, though thin
has purity, and I begin
to sense an emptiness within
which something is waiting.

The Ovi is a folk rhythm and consists of three lines of eight syllables
rhyming with each other and a fourth unrhymed and slightly shorter
line.

MONGOLIAN

Sometimes

Sometimes a gesture....
  how she sheds her coat.
Sometimes a sound....
  her footstep on the stair.
Sometimes an absence....
  one hair on the pillow.
Sometimes a syllable,
  her half-heard answer.

Sometimes a colour....
  crimson at her throat.
Sometimes a pause....
  her hand upon the door.
Sometimes time itself,
  slow ticking time
sums up all answers
  I am hunting for.

The poem is composed of quatrains, each line front-rhyming with the next. The rhymes are composed of complete syllables. Internal alliteration is frequent. The line length is not laid down but is usually of 7 or 8 syllables. There should be three or four stresses in each line.

In this example I have chosen to indent the second half of each line to emphasize the caesura.

OCCITAN

Idee Fixe

I have no other thought
than of her loveliness
that drives me to distress
each time I pay her court.
I have no other thought.

My tongue cannot express
the way her ways obsess
until I am distraught;
I have no other thought

than that she may say Yes,
permit some small caress;
rebellious flesh grows taut.
I have no other thought,

no other dream to bless
my nights with hopefulness
but passion cuts it short.
I have no other thought;

no cause, no creed possess
my mind but this princess
whose grace is Goddess-taught;
I have no other thought,

unable to digress,
my studies futureless
and all my learning naught;
I have no other thought.

This Occitan (or Provençal) form has no set metre, but I have chosen a six syllable line as this is common in Occitan verse. The first line is also the concluding line of the first stanza of five lines and of all the following four line stanzas, the rhyme scheme being: A B B A A B B A A B B A A B B A A and so on.

OLD NORSE

DROTTKVAETT

Workshop

Rustling berried bushes,
  birds once heard singing
slide in hiding shadows,
  shuffle, scuttle, filling
leaves with little trembles,
  twitching twigs, inventing
tunes we'll feel as supple
  songs for summer's ending.

The Drottkvaett is composed in quatrains, with six syllables in each half line. Each half line contains three stressed and three unstressed syllables and concludes with a trochee. One example could be: ˘ ́ ˘ ́ ́ ˘. Another could be simply trochaic trimeter: ́ ˘ ́ ˘ ́ ˘.

Usually the even lines are fully rhymed and the odd ones are near rhymed with assonance. The lines are linked together in pairs by assonance. This is a Skaldic metre.

FORNYROISLAG

O Tempora

Time torments us,
  teases with wars,

frustrates freedoms,
    flippant; as flames
consume empires,
    make the skies dark,
clocks, all uncaring,
    click ticking on.

The Fornyroislag is an Eddic metre. There are four lines in a stanza, each line being composed of two parts, each of which contains four or five syllables.

    Metre: there are two stressed syllables in each half line and two or three unstressed. A possible metre would be: ´ ˘ ´ ˘ * ´ ˘ ˘ ´ and another ˘ ´ ˘ ˘ ´ * ˘ ´ ˘ ´ ˘.

    The verse is bound together by alliteration. In the first half line the alliterating sound may be placed anywhere; in the second half line the alliteration falls on the first stressed syllable.

HRYNHENT

Riverside

Underneath the rain-grey heavens
where the sparse reeds bow and shiver,
the shadowing bronze trees' descending
leaves lie still upon the river,
held apart from scurrying currents
by some need of dreaming water
to retain the fall's remembrance,
guard against the warning future.

The Hrynhent is a Skaldic metre and differs from the Drottkvaett only in possessing two additional syllables in the form of trochees, one in each half line.

After the Rain

Bleak of beak,
  birds in meadows
stooping, stab;
  we watch, saddened,
harsh hunger,
  earth-harassing,
wild, wanton,
  wish for singing.

The Kviouhattr is a Skaldic metre, each line being made up of two half lines with the syllable count 3 4. There are two stresses in each half line. Thus one line might run: ´˘´ * ˘´˘´. It could equally well run: ˘´´ * ´˘˘´. The poem is bound together by alliteration.

In the Olympics

Clustering, calm,
  the clouds possess
our morning mountain, hide
cavern and crag,
  commanding dawn
to learn love's gentleness.

The Ljoahattr is an Eddic metre. It is composed in quatrains, the first and third lines containing 4 or 5 syllables. The second and fourth lines are shorter. The first and third lines have a caesura; the second and fourth lines do not.

There is no endrhyme, but the first half of the first and third lines alliterate with the second half, as with the Fornyroislag. The shorter second and fourth lines have internal alliteration.

A possible metrical pattern would be:

/ ˘ ˘ / * ˘ / ˘ /
˘ / ˘ / ˘ /
/ ˘ ˘ / * ˘ / ˘ /
˘ / /   / ˘ ˘

MALAHATTR
_____

The Fir

This tree, a towering
   triumphant solitude,
murmurous, is making
   a music that alters
the dream and the dreamer,
   denying reality,
reviving the vanishing
   vistas of prophecy.

The Malahattr is an Eddic metre. The lines have ten or 12 syllables and are divided into half lines containing two stressed and three or four unstressed syllables. The half lines are connected by alliteration.

A possible metrical pattern would be: ˘ / ˘ / ˘ ˘ * / ˘ ˘ / ˘ ˘.

Crows in the Oak Bay

Our oak is black
with crows that clack
their beaks and caw.
About a score
are gathered, stiff
and gaunt, as if
all waiting till
we die, or kill.

The Runnhent is a Skaldic metre, and has four syllables in each line. The metre is iambic dimeter: ˘ ´ ˘ ´. This may, however, vary so that feminine rhymes can occur. There must always be two stresses, however. Thus one variant could be: ˘ ´ ˘ ´ ˘ and another ´ ˘ ´ ˘ .

PERSIAN

Hurricane

The storm-swept town of sun-scarred stone
   beside green lakes now finds huge waves
of green rear tall to crash sea walls,
   engulf broad streets and pile tides high.

The townsfolk ask the rock-torn shore,
   the down-hurled walls, the grey skies, "Who?"
There's no far word from dark-eyed gods
   to tell storm's ways or why men die.

The Hazaj metre is composed of lines of 32 syllables divided into two hemistiches (or halves) of 16 syllables each. These hemistiches are of four feet with the rhythm ⌣ ⁄ ⁄ ⁄ ⌣ ⁄ ⁄ ⁄ ⌣ ⁄ ⁄ ⁄ ⌣ ⁄ ⁄ ⁄ . In the above verse I have indented the second half of each hemistich; thus each stanza is in fact one line of verse. This Hajaz metre differs from the Arabic Hajaz metre in having 16 rather than twelve syllables in each half line.

Leaf Requiem

The dawn light is grey, chill; I turn over, stare;

my pale window's made music, changed vision, shown
a leaf pinned by night rain and bronze-gold on air:
a small death can sound anthems, pierce breath and bone.

Mathnavi means simply a rhyming couplet. The mutaqarib metre
has 22 syllables in each line, which is divided into two hemistiches
of eleven syllables each. Each hemistich has four feet with the
rhythm ∪∕∕ ∪∕∕ ∪∕∕ ∪∕. This metre, like many Persian metres,
is Arabic in origin.

Mujtass Metre

Ghazal for Saki

To lounge at ease in the cool shade beneath the leaves of
    the vine
  and pour one's love a full cup of crimson pleasuring
      wine,
to take the hand of a new love and wander into a bar,
  the pulse and heart of an old inn and find the
      Burgundy fine,

To lay abed in the sweet hour when wine and loving are
      strong,
  to bring the spirit a new strength, the poem a
      surprising line,
to kiss a girl on the soft lips and find her willingness
      clear,
  her beauty more than a mere lure as chance and
      darkness combine,

to lift a glass to an old friend with gladness, dinner ahead
    with other friends on a feast night as candles, radiant,
        shine,
to drink, to drink as the years pass, from goblet, chalice,
    or glass
    with love, to love and in good heart; these resolutions
        are mine.

A Ghazal is composed of rhyming couplets all on the same rhyme, the subject matter being conventionally love and wine. There should, ideally, be five to fifteen couplets.

    The Mujtass metre is composed in lines of thirty syllables divided into two hemistiches or half lines of fifteen syllables. The rhythm of the half line is in four feet: ◡–◡– ◡◡–– ◡–◡– ◡◡–. The opening two half lines rhyme with each other as here.

MUZARI METRE

Goldstream Climax

Bright salmon challenge torrents
    of wild water, spill their seed,
die, crimson staining pebbles,
    the chill river blessing need.

The Muzari metre is composed of two lines of 14 syllables each, forming a Mathnavi, or rhymed couplet. The rhythmical pattern is
––◡ –◡–◡ ◡–◡– ◡–.

Street Scene

Walking warm streets summer rain makes shine,
   her lithe young body charms
lifting full skirts over pools, head bent;
   the round sun licks her heel;
ancient, rayed hair blazing light, pulse fast,
   he, great god, almost cries,
begging bright clear eyes to gaze sky-high,
   accept heat's old appeal.

The Ramal metre is composed in lines of 30 syllables divided into two half lines of 15 syllables each. The half lines are of four feet, the rhythm being ╱◡╱╱ ╱◡╱╱ ╱◡╱╱ ╱◡╱. In this verse I have indented the second half of each hemistich after the ninth syllable to make the overall rhythm clearer.

   The Persian Ramal metre differs from the Arabic one by having four feet in each hemistich rather than three.

Winter

Winter bears down hard on old earth's broken stones,
   brings out white hoar frost to hide breaks, bruises,
      scars,
asking why mere men destroy time's gentle bones,
   piles the snowdrifts high beneath night's watching
      stars,

weighs the bare boughs down with soft swathed comfort,
    sighs,
mourning mankind's need to log, plough, quarry, flay,
smothers all harsh sounds machines make near and far,
sending whiplash winds to keep Spring's lusts at bay.

This version of the Ramal metre is composed in lines of 22 syllables divided into two halves or hemistiches of eleven syllables each. The rhythm of each hemistich is ′ ⌣ ′ ′   ′ ⌣ ′ ′   ′ ⌣ ′. This is the metre in which Rumi's *Mathnavi* (meaning couplets) was written. In this example I have broken the lines into their hemistiches, each stanza thus forming a couplet.

R U B A I

Night Thoughts

Sometimes in the deep of night the mind wearily sways,
dazed, drunken with love, with wine, with black thoughts
    as it strays
lost, wandering through the forest's dreamtime, and
    alone,
blind, fearing the wines, the loves, that bring death to our
    days.

The Rubai is a quatrain with the rhyme scheme A A B A, or sometimes, A A A A. The metre of the Rubai is in lines of thirteen (or twelve) syllables with the rhythm ′ ′ ⌣   ⌣ ′ ⌣ ′   ⌣ ′ ′   ⌣ ⌣ ′ (or ′ ′). A Rubaijat is a gathering of such quatrains, but not necessarily as a sequence. Fitzgerald's version of Omar Khayyam follows the rhyme scheme of the original, but not its metre, and creates a kind of sequence from quatrains which do not form one in the original text.

PRAKRIT

Crawlspace

In the warm darkness beneath home
as the feet thumped loudly above crouched boyhood,
earth spirits murmured old truths
I understood with an unspoiled trust and love.

Prakrit is a language closely related to Sanskrit and the Arya metre is that of the poems of the *Sattasai*, each of which is written in a slightly different version of the metre. The main principle of regularity appears to be the number of feet in a line; the Arya metre is composed of quatrains of 3, 4, 3 and 4 feet. The above verse follows the metre of the second poem of the Sattasai as scanned by George L. Hart III in his book *The Poems of Ancient Tamil* (University of California Press, 1975). The metre runs as follows:

⏑⏑´ ⏑´´ ´´
⏑⏑´ ´´ ⏑´⏑´ ´´
´´ ⏑´⏑ ´´
⏑´⏑ ´⏑⏑ ⏑´´⏑ ´

RUSSIAN

Dolnik

Dawn

In the pallid light of the dawn
the unknown becomes a despair
as the questioning starts again
with its who and its why and where
and the grasses shake in the air
for Reason has been reborn
from a dream and is bruised and bare
and the curtain of time is torn.

The Dolnik is composed in lines of eight syllables with the rhythm
˘ ˘ ′ ˘ ′ ˘ ˘ ′ or ˘ ˘ ′ ˘ ˘ ′ ˘ ′. Additional uncounted syllables
may sometimes follow the eighth syllable which carries the rhyme.

Onegin Stanza

On the Beach

The block of stone upon the shore,
a home for gathered sand and weed,
a useless object left by war,
recalls beleaguered pride and need.
The sea that eats away our land

and holds our houses broken, drowned,
with clear horizons, breakers calm,
today suggest no coming harm,
but, walking sands that drift and silt
to wind and wave I know that years
will bring again the threat, the fears,
that cliffs will fall and blood be spilt;
though hopes and dreams may comfort us,
the sands of time are ominous.

The Onegin Stanza was invented by Pushkin for his *Eugene Onegin*. It has 14 lines of iambic tetrameter (˘ ´ ˘ ´ ˘ ´ ˘ ´) with the rhyme scheme A B A B C C D D E F F E G G.

SANSKRIT

Listening

As we listen
to green leaves in
their recurrence
of rustling, then
to the sudden
and still pause, we
are becoming
a dream of birds.

The Anustubh Metre has sixteen syllables in each line of a two line verse.

Considerable freedom is given to the composer in this metre, some syllables being described as neither long nor short; they could be either. I have given these syllables the notation - . The metre therefore is ---- ◡ ⁄ ⁄ - --⁄ - ◡ ⁄ ◡ -.

Sanskrit verse does not usually rhyme but there may be assonance and consonance within the lines.

DRUTAVILAMBITA METRE

Into the Depths

Into the deeps of the ocean I sent my dream

in a belief that its wanderings would find more
than those of reason whose visions display no gleam,
and from the ocean my shadow returned to shore.

The Drutavilambita Metre has 12 syllables in each line. The metre
is ⌣⌣⌣ʹ ⌣⌣ʹ ⌣⌣ʹ ⌣ʹ. There are instances of end rhyme in
Kalidasa's *Vikramorvasiya* which is composed in this metre; I have,
therefore, felt permitted to use rhyme myself.

INDRAVAJIRA/UPENDRAVAJIRA METRE

Snapshot

For Jill Solnicki

The lonely child slouching across the playground,
his eyes on scuffed shoes and his glasses broken,
is phrasing fame's name in his head and hiding
his wanton wild songs till tomorrows beckon.

The Indravajira/Upendravajira Metre has eleven syllables in each
line. As in the Anustubh metre, some syllables are left to the dis-
cretion of the composer to stress or leave unstressed and these syllables are marked -. The rhythm is: -ʹ⌣ ʹʹ⌣ ʹ⌣ ʹ⌣ -. As before
I have separated the long and short syllables into "feet" to make it
easier to perceive the pattern.

Sleeping Out, New Delhi

The warm earth's breath in the night
    sighs as sleepers sigh
their way through sleep, and the stars,
    overhead, reply
with slow far gestures of grief,
    understanding why
all creatures troubled by time
    need a means to die.

The Jakati metre consists of a line of 12 syllables in three parts, these having the rhythm, (- standing for syllables that may be long or short, stressed or unstressed) -ʹ -ʹ * -ˇ - * ʹ ˇ ʹ ˇ -. I have arranged the above lines with the two parts forming one unit and the third another in order to make the construction more observable.

SARDULA-VIKRIDITA METRE

Time Sleeps

Time dreams under the apple tree, is at peace.
    No thought of man's troubles intrudes.
Hour-glass, scythe, and entangling beard are mislaid.
    Off duty, Time smiles in his sleep.
Some say love is his dream, but others have doubts;
    some think he's lost heart and retired,
bored stiff, wearied by numbers, measurements, years.

Shake, wake him; Death's blessing is lost.

The Sardula metre is composed in lines of 19 syllables, the first half line being of 11 syllables and the second of eight. The metrical pattern is: ´´ ´˘˘ ´˘´ ´´˘ * ´´ ˘´ ´˘ ˘´. I have separated the long and short syllables into groups that constitute classical "feet" to make it easier to perceive a pattern.

TRISTUBH METRE

By the Wall

For Rona Murray

The old man squats
  by the wall,
    a twisted tree.
The crumbling wall
  has been hacked
    by years and birds,
by scraping claws,
  by despairs,
    by hopes and vows.
The old man nods
  in a place
    that time has made
for such as he
  and the sun
    allows him shade
and coins collect
  at his feet,
    not many coins

and less than bright,
   but the dream
      is more than this,
for standing tall
   in his mind
      the god he knows
his own has said
   that the wheel
      is moving round.
The old man leans
   on the wall
      and waits for song.

The Tristubh Metre is composed in lines of three parts and the rhythmic shape (‑ standing for a syllable that may be heavy or light) follows the pattern ‑ʹ‑ʹ * ˘˘ʹ * ˘ʹ˘‑.

SPANISH

COPLA DE ARTE MAYOR

Sleepless

Awake in the darkness, aware of her sleeping,
I wonder if dreamers can send on a message
to different sleepers, if nightmares can damage
a stranger with terrors that others are shaping,
and, all of a sudden, I find I am hoping
that nobody's vision becomes an intruder
on anyone's journey; the freedom to wander
alone is the only one left in our keeping.

The Copla de Arte Mayor is an eight line stanza, the lines being of 12 syllable in two hemistiches or halves of six syllables each.

The rhyme scheme is A B B A A C C A. Other acceptable rhyme schemes are A B A B B C C B, and A B B A A C A C. The metre is
ᵕ ´ ᵕ ᵕ ´ ᵕ * ᵕ ´ ᵕ ᵕ ´ ᵕ. This could be described as amphibrachic tetrameter.

CUECA CHILENA

The End of It

The house where I was a young
student has found rest,
tile and brick that held it up

gone, leaving it blest,
yes, leaving it blest,
unshackled and free
of time and space, forgotten
all that history.

Its old rooms gather round me
wherever my bed,
recalling all that has been,
reclaiming my dead,
yes, claiming my dead
that gaze from the past
I wear as I wear my clothes,
old, patched, made to last.

Today, although seated here
in my study room
I'm also under that roof
wondering to whom,
yes, asking to whom
as the night descends
I'll send out my memories
of those long lost friends.

This is a dance song of South America, and consists of a seguidilla
with an additional line, a repetition of the fourth one, beginning
with (in Spanish) the word *Sí*. The metre is that of the seguidilla,
the number of syllables in each stanza being 7 5 7 5 5 5 7 5. A
change of mood occurs after the fifth line which in essence re-
places the caesura or break of the seguidilla. The rhyme scheme (or
pattern of assonance in the original) is A B C B B D E D.

On a June Evening

A pair of raccoons have climbed
  high into the cherry tree;
beside the fence in the dusk,
  narrowing our eyes to see
sharp noses, masks, peering down
  on us, the intruders, we
wait for them both to descend
  assured in temerity.

They scramble clumsily down
  impervious to our stares;
they are bland desperadoes
  knowing that nobody cares
to challenge them or dispute
  their presence, for our affairs
too use the edge of darkness
  and our hands reach out like theirs.

Cuaderna Via (also called alejandrino, nueva maestria, mester de clerecia) is composed in monorhymed quatrains, each line being made up of two, seven syllable halves or hemistiches. The end rhymes should also consonate with each other. The syllable count and rhyme scheme are thus:

Syllables: 14 14 14 14
Rhymes: A   A   A   A

To Liam Miller

I never dreamed you could die,
you, the pulse of my story,
those vast unwritten volumes
dependent on your devious shrewd memory.

What use is a curt footnote,
a poised point of reference
directing readers elsewhere
to uncover subtleties of pretence?

There's no elsewhere effective
as your slow knowing smile,
your spread hands indicating
the little ellipses that pass scholars by,

voids I, too, have forgotten,
idolatries of the blood,
pauses on Dublin street corners,
visions and revisions that never made good.

But now with, I think, a smile
you have lifted a dead weight
from my hunched scribbling shoulder,
allowing me to continue to forget

embarrassments of detail
and simply, with love, recall
you my friend and mentor
who showed me the way to climb over the wall.

The Endecha found its established form in the sixteenth century and though there are variations it is now generally agreed that it is composed in quatrains and that the formula is as follows:

Syllables: 7 7 7 11
Rhymes: A B C B

The rhymes are most frequently consonance, but full rhymes are not outlawed.

ESPINELA

Laburnum

The tall laburnum by the wall
drops twisted yellow petals, and,
as if caught up in distant sound,
they dance with sunlight as they fall.

Each Spring these dancing shapes enthrall,
but then with different eyes we see
slim dry seed-clusters hanging free
above our burdened earth and know
when music's done we stand below
the quiet of a killing tree.

The Espinela is composed of ten octosyllabic lines with a break after the fourth, and the rhyme scheme is: A B B A * A C C D D C. It is named after the poet Vicentre Espinel (1550-1524) who is credited with inventing it.

Nocturne

For Ludwig Zeller and Susana Wold

Musicians in twilight
form harmonies to bring
love's far darkness near
as their instruments play
on the heart's hidden string.

Listeners at evening
feel the darkness enfold
all thought in a cloak
as profound as the sea
and as timelessly old.

But dancers in darkness
ride out on the bars,
being, not playing
or hearing the music,
and are pierced by the stars.

The Flamenca (also called Playera and Seguidilla Gitana) is composed in stanzas of five lines, the second and fifth lines being in
assonance. The third and fourth lines may be combined if desired.
    Syllables: 6 6 5 6 6
    End Rhymes: A B C D B

The Forge at Sundown

Embers and anvil
serve the old ways.
Sunset remembers
the Ancient of Days

as the spear-maker,
the shaper of swords,
the falsehood-breaker,
the wielder of words

on the black metal
where promises bound
both spirit and will
in the hammer sound.

Twilight has ended;
the fireball sun
in the West's descended,
but Fire burns on

and, red in the heart
of our darkness, gleams
on craft and on art
and our iron dreams.

The Folia is a short-lined poem in quatrains with the rhyme scheme
A B A B.

The Memories

Texte by Lawrence Olson

These I remember in the dark,
Voices, a touch of hands, a cry,
The Sunday concert in the park,
And how we live and how we die.

Peter who flew and flew just high
enough for Death to find its mark,
and Eve who dare not pause to cry;
these I remember in the dark

and Wilfred lettering like God's clerk
poems that the world-mad hurried by,
and John discovered hanged and stark —
voices, a touch of hands, a cry

of pain, of pleasure, and a sigh.
The weekly hop, the drunken lark,
the skinny-dip, stars far and sly,
the Sunday concert in the park,

all's over, done, yet I embark
each night on memories to try
and comprehend our primal spark
and how we live and how we die.

The Glose opens with a quotation from another author, which is
then repeated as refrain to succeeding verses, line by line. Gleeson
White stated that the opening quotation (or texte) should be a
quatrain and that it should be followed by four ten-line stanzas,

these stanzas rhyming on the sixth, ninth and tenth lines. Other authorities do not give these restrictions but only state that the texte must be repeated, line by line, as refrain for the following verses. The quatrain form of the texte is not considered essential.

LIRA

Dawn Meadow

In my neighbouring meadow
the light is a line of mist,
a kind of silver shadow,
chill, shimmering. Where we kissed
the light is a line of mist.

I should not make much of this.
It is dawn's usual way
and nothing has gone amiss.
If distances blur and sway
it is dawn's usual way.

The mist is melting to day;
a silken wisp on the ground
still glimmers but will not stay.
Was that all the truth we found,
a silken wisp on the ground,

a passing pleasure, a sound
of music lovely and far
with nothing hedging us round,
each moment murmured a bar
of music lovely and far

though never to come too near?
We both of us understood
how happiness beckons fear;
that nothing is wholly good
we both of us understood.

Yet maybe we could and should....
The mist has drifted and gone
away from the place we stood;
now that the day has begun
the mist has drifted and gone.

The Lira is a poem composed of four, five, or six line stanzas, the lines being either seven or 11 syllables long. The second line in the five line form is repeated as the fifth line. There is no set metre. The rhyme scheme runs: A B A B B.

M O T E

Amherst October

For David R. Clark

In Autumn sumac is remembrance
red as a king's red robes.

The Mote is subject to no rules as to syllable count or metre. A mote is a two line poem that forms a complete sentence.

A Question Of Definition

Q. Can this be love —
   her fingers caressing my sleeve?
Can this be love,
   the slow drawing on of her glove
when it seems she just *must* leave,
with a smile I long to believe?
Can this be love?

A. They call it love:
   the subtle suggestion, the guile.
They call it love,
   that sweet word to be wary of
even if offered with a smile.
We rhapsodize, then we revile;
they call it love.

In the Pregunta a question (requesta) is asked by one poet and the answer (respuesta) is provided by another, using precisely the same verse form and rhyme scheme. Practiced by the poets of the court in the late fourteenth and fifteenth centuries the topic was often love, but also morality, religion, and philosophy. These stanzas are Rondelets.

Question Time

For Walter de la Mare

Who are you?
   I don't know.
Grass when the winds blow,

Who am I?
   I can't say.
Waves where the winds play.

What's this place?
   I can't tell.
Mirror and miracle.

See previous note. This example follows a pattern used by Herrick.

Spring Dawn

There is a sharp edge to the day's
beginnings and the chestnut trees,
wind-sliced, are troubled in their praise
as each piled candle tilts and sways
dismayed by morning's heresies.

The Quintilla is a five line stanza with eight syllable lines and uti-
lizing two rhyming sounds, which may be cases of consonance.
The possible rhyme schemes are A B A A B (as here) and A B A B A,
A B B A B, A A B A B, A A B B A.

REDONDILLA

The Afternoon

This bird completes the afternoon;
perched on the lichen-scribbled fence,
it brings the pleasures of suspense:
it may or may not pipe a tune.

Other components of the scene
are less ambiguous; the grass
breathes steadily as hours pass;
the garden roller, a serene

brown presence, is an iron god,
a solid, potent, deity;
the foxgloves, spiring splendidly
beside the laurel, sway and nod,

but yet without this bird the whole
would not imply the possible,
the sly "perhaps," the visible
and outward sign of how the soul

is balanced on the edge of time
poised both for song and sudden flight
as eyelids may change day for night
and speechless flowers choose to mime

the shifting rhetorics of our play;
the afternoon's become complete,
and, feathers fluffing to the heat,
the bird is free to fly away.

The Redondilla is composed of octosyllabic quatrains rhyming A B
B A.

S c u l p s i t

Having made this bird of stone
black as a black pool
at evening under trees
and cleaned each edged tool,
I lay supper things
out on my scarred scrubbed table
hear night's beating wings.

The Seguidilla is a seven line poem or stanza that emerged from
earlier verse forms and became established as having a definite
change of direction after the fourth line and having the following
formula.
Syllables: 7 5 7 5 * 5 7 5
End Rhymes: A B C B   D B D
The rhymes are usually more instances of consonance than full
rhymes.

Filey Brigg Revisited

For Christopher Wiseman

We trod the narrow rocky track
between the mounds of bladderwrack
shadowed by the cliff's black height
around the brigg that edged the bay;
the sea was satin-smooth that day,
the sky unnaturally bright.

Out on the point where shelves of rock
descended step by step, he took
the rod from its brown canvas case,
assembled it, cast, reeled in, cast,
and sluggishly the minutes passed.
I clambered to another place.

The cavern that I found near by
was empty; half its roof was sky
and for its floor it had a pool
I sidled round from ledge to ledge
to squat upon its weed-green edge,
and the whole sky was in that pool.

Within its infinite depthless blue
were fish that swam as if they flew
through magical mysterious air,
a dozen of them, swerving, thin
and black, their eyes like shiny tin
impervious to my boyhood stare.

They moved in perfect unison;
the leading fish would turn, and on
the instant all of them would turn,
complete companions in a way
I'd not envisaged till that day
and knew that I would never learn.

I wished I'd brought a shrimping net,
for then I could have reached them — yet
I liked their independent look,
seeming so confident and sure
their cavern sky kept them secure
from any human net or hook.

An adult might have had the sense
to laugh at them for innocence,
they were so free, assured, and small;
myself, I felt and shared their pride,
then shivered, for the rising tide
I knew would soon engulf them all.

That pool would vanish in the shock
of breakers battering the rock;
lost in the vastness of the sea
they would be swept out of their sky
and find no other place to fly.
I felt the sea engulfing me.

I jumped up from my weed-green seat
and left the place on stumbling feet
possessed by unfamiliar fear;
my father stood there, blond and tall;
there was no need to fear at all.
But now the tide is drawing near.

The Sextilla is a poem in six line stanzas, the lines usually being of eight syllables. The most generally accepted rhyme scheme is A A B C C B as above, but other acceptable formulae are A B A B C C. In earlier days there were numerous different rhyme schemes, almost all of them utilizing two rhymes rather than three.

S OLEDAD

In July

Gently the magnolia sways
its polished leaves, rephrasing all
the mirrorings of summer days.

The Soledad is a poem or stanza of three, eight syllable lines rhyming A B A with some internal consonance and assonance.

Z EJEL

In Age

When age begins to gently murmur
words like haven, home, and harbour,
also it needs must remember.

It is not the obvious comes
marching up with pipes and drums,
not great banquets but dropped crumbs
that seize the time to whisper.

The wounded bird my boyhood held
warm in the hand, heart pulsing, wild,
with gaping beak, trapped as a child,
I think will throb for ever.

The velvet on my mother's gown
before she took the steep stairs down
from bedtime to some night unknown
still touches me with wonder.

My father, tall against the bright
spring sky, and flying my box kite
so high I thought space infinite,
defines both pride and splendour.

As death draws near I do not yearn
to live it all again, return
to any place I've been, but learn
to guide what I remember.

The Zejel is a Spanish form opening with a rhyming triplet called a mudanza. This is followed by quatrains composed of a triplet followed by a line rhyming with the mudanza thus: AAA BBBA CCCA and so on. The metre is most frequently octosyllabic, but this is not a hard and fast rule.

SUMERIAN

Her Beauty

She is as beautiful as hands
   moving to music,
slim fingered hands with polished nails
   caressing harp strings
or discovering in the air
   invisible shapes
the music offers our silence:
   wings above water,
leaf turning to leaf as day ends,
   a petal falling;
she is as beautiful as time
   when lovers murmur
under the trees by the river
   where white swans gather.

This form cannot be more than hypothetical. We know that some Sumerian verse was constructed of lines alternating eight and five syllables and that it made some occasional use of alliteration and assonant chiming, but that is all we know. This example is, therefore, constructed of 13 syllable lines divided into eight and five. Sumerian verse, like Egyptian and Hebrew verse, is also characterized by parallelism and apposition.

SWAHILI

Conch

Not thinking of mind's grasp or reach,
I come upon a spiralled shell
white in the piled weed of the beach;
from childhood I have known these tell
my ears of sounding tides and teach
the dooms tumultuous breakers spell
out in their spindrift, for by well
hurled climax passion is defined

and limited; it cannot last;
the sounding shell itself is dead,
the life that shaped its chambers past.
Remembering this, discomfited,
I pick it up and hold it fast
so not to hear how history's bred
mere echoes echoing, the lost
and hollow sound of humankind.

This verse form has no established name. I have given it the name of its most distinguished practitioner, Muyaka bin Haji al-Ghassaniy, of Mombassa. It consists of stanzas composed of eight, eight syllable hemistichs (or half lines) with the rhyme scheme A B A B A B B C. The c rhyme is repeated as the ending of the last line in all the stanzas.

T A M I L

Outside the Village

Dark trees in the night wood breathe heavily,
deep roots probing into the earth's fundament,
as the white moon rises above
the disturbed sharp leaves, black boughs, huge boles.

The Aciriyappa metre is made up of lines of four feet. These four feet are either kinds of Akavarkir or kinds of Vencir. The akavarkir feet are: ´´ ˘˘´ ´˘˘ ˘˘˘˘ . The Vencir metre differs only in having an additional stressed syllable. The scansion of the above example is:

```
´´        ˘˘´   ´´      ´˘˘
´´        ´˘˘   ˘˘´     ´˘˘
˘˘´   ´´         ˘˘´
˘˘´   ´´    ´´        ´´
```

The third line here has only three feet, which is a frequent variation.

Bubbles

Where the stones in the stream force water to turbulence
there are bright bubbles restating the tall truths of the

rainbow:
as they scatter their thin-skinned radiance, memory,
like a fish leaping, delights in a sky shaped by the mind's
   eye.

The Kali metre or Kalippa is composed in lines of four feet, each line most commonly beginning with a nirai foot of two unstressed syllables, and also frequently ending with the same foot. The scansion of the above consists of two lines repeated thus:

˘ ˘ ´   ˘ ˘ ´ ´   ´ ˘ ˘   ´ ˘ ˘
˘ ˘ ´ ´   ˘ ˘ ´   ˘ ˘ ´ ´   ˘ ˘ ´ ´

Venpa Metre

The Dreams

Dreams challenging time are an unexplored country of
   truths,
far memories wandering the intense spaces between
bring visions and fantasies that we know sent by our
   dead,
kind spirits that counsel us.

The Venpa metre is usually presented in two to four lines, all but the final line having four feet; it has three. The scansion of the above is as follows. The first three lines run ´ ´   ˘ ˘ ´   ˘ ˘ ˘ ˘ ´   ´ ˘ ˘ ´ and the fourth line has the rhythm ´ ´   ˘ ˘ ´   ˘ ˘.

T H A I

The Poet Confesses

As I bend to my theme,
  as I bend to my verse,
I am lost to the sense
  of the words that I shape
on the page, for her eyes
  are the shine of the ink
and the breath of her lips
  is the hush of the brush.

The Totok is composed of four lines of 12 syllables, each 12 syllable line having the rhythm ⌣ ⌣ ⁄ ⌣ ⌣ ⁄ ⌣ ⌣ ⁄ ⌣ ⌣ ⁄, which could be described as an anapestic tetrameter. Rhyme is not required.

TIBETAN

Gzha

Spring Lament

All the snow is departed;
days are growing lonely;
all the hills are greening;
no chill holds her housebound.

The Gzha is a dance song and the form is that of a quatrain with four lines of six syllables each and frequently in trochaic metre as here (´˘ ´˘ ´˘) though the last line commences with a spondee (´ ´). There is no rhyme required, but parallelism is expected and some internal consonance and assonance.

VIETNAMESE

Nightsong

When moonlight stains the leaf
solitude stares at grief till dawn.

The Luc-Bat is a six syllable line followed by an eight syllable line,
the sixth syllable of each line rhyming.

Her Face

When she turned her small head
towards me in the red sunset
I was sure we had met
long ago in a better place
than this cold town, her face.
A dream I could not trace, had lost
somewhere on some far coast
in the east or the west of things.
I did not speak. Age stings.
Sometimes remembering is cursed.

This form of Luc-Bat connects each couplet in which the sixth syllable of each line rhymes with the next line that then has two extra syllables; the connection takes the form of rhyming the usually unrhymed eighth syllable with the sixth syllable of the next couplet. John Balaban, in his book *Ca Dao Vietnam* (Unicorn Press, 1980), tells us that he recorded this variation on October, 1971 in the Mekong Delta, the singer, and possibly the originator of the form, being Mrs. Bui Thi Cu, who was at that time seventy-three years old.

WELSH

One characteristic of Welsh verse is impossible to reproduce all accurately in English. This is the technique Cynghanedd, which has been divided into four kinds. A simple description of the main principles of each is as follows:

Cynghanedd Groes

The consonants in the first half of the line are repeated in the second and in the same order.

Cynghanedd Draws

A form of Cyghanedd Groes in which the middle syllables of the line are left out of consideration, the repeated consonants being given after this.

Cynghanedd Sain

The line is divided into three parts, the first two of which rhyme. The rhyming syllable of the second part is linked to the third part by consonance or alliteration.

Cynghanedd Lusg

This can only be used in lines that end with an unaccented syllable if it is not to interfere with the pattern of end rhymes. A syllable in the first half of the line rhymes with the stressed penultimate syllable of the line.

There are many subtleties in "Cynghanedd" and a great deal of attention has been paid to subdivisions of the various categories. Some poems have mixed the kinds together in a line of verse and these mixtures have been given names. The subject was taken so seriously that some forms of Cynghanedd were actually prohibited in 1450 at the Carmarthen Eisteddfod.

While not utilizing Cynghanedd in the following poems, I have followed the principles upon which it is based and made constant use of internal consonance, rhyme, and alliteration.

Awdl Gywydd

Dawn Mist

When white mist drifts from the sea
and we hear the foghorn sound
through the grey skein of the dawn
something's born upon the strand;

something's born and something dies
beside the twisting lines of foam;
pebbles shining wetly bright,
morning light exhales and moans.

Nothing here is safe from change;
shapes shift, alter; thought is dead;
touch is nerveless; dreams are spurned;
love turns over in the bed.

Sun may burn through mist, but we'll
still feel coldness, having met
this, the breath that whispered earth
and birth and death and can't forget.

The Awdl Gywydd has the formula:
Syllables: 7 7 7 7
End rhymes: A B C B

End words A and C rhyme the third, fourth or fifth syllable in the lines immediately following.

Byr a Thoddaid

After the Storm

I do not wish to think of war
but yesterday, outside, I saw
a branch of blossom broken by the wind
stretched ruined to the sky.

It was enough to send me back
to boyhood when the nights were black
except for searchlights crossing beams way high
above my restless dreams.

enough to stand me in the town
to watch a torn house crumble down
to rubble and to dust that made eyes smart,
heart hurt, and mind afraid,

enough to make me think of one
as tall as Springtime who flew on
beyond our boundaries in youth and pride
and was denied time's truth.

Great wars grow meaningless at last,
a part of the absurd far past
or scraps of history, little more, except
for us who have kept score,

not of slogan, flag and deed
but of the little wounds that bleed
so quietly we'd think them whole but for
the sore place in the soul

that troubles us whenever we
see broken toy or shattered tree
with tattered blossoms scattered by the wind
beneath a ruined sky.

Byr A Thoddaid has the formula:
    Syllables: 8 8 10 6
    End rhymes: A A B B
The first of the B rhymes actually occurs before the end of the
line, frequently on the eighth syllable, and the syllables following it
are echoed by rhyme, consonance, or alliteration with the first syllables of the last line.

CLOGYRNACH

Again and Again

The tales must be told and retold,
the quick mountain river run cold
through each ancient song
to which we belong,
sharing longings of old.

Each time the theme rises and dies
all earth rediscovers its cries
and cavern and tree
their dark ancestry

with its freedoms and lies.

Those few that renew the heart's fee
reborn and remade grow to be
their own selves no more
but words of earth lore
that explore, bind, and free.

The Glogyrnach has the formula:
    Syllables: 8 8 5 5 3 3
    End rhymes: A A B B B A
    The last two lines are often written as one.

Cyhydedd Fer

The Log

I walked across the frosty lawn.
A log of timber, newly sawn,
was leant against a withered tree;
I don't suppose you'd ever see
a thing less beautiful, and yet
because the bark was raw and wet,
and perhaps because the sky was bright,
it broke into my mind tonight.

The Cyhydedd Fer is composed in couplets:
    Syllables: 8 8
    End rhymes: A A
    As with all couplet forms, it is not necessary to regard each
couplet as a separate stanza.

The Decision

For Fenris

It is time to break
the grip of the book,
snap its bitter lock,
dissolve its chain;
it is time to turn
to the spellbound fern,
to words of the burn
on the mountain,

for that long-held law
brought us little more
than a bolted door
and a drawn blind,
while, huddled within
thick walls we have been
neither kith nor kin
or even friend

to the lives that share
our earth and our air,
oak, hemlock and fir,
hawk, eagle, crow,
though each living thing —
fur, flower, fin, wing,
is more than showing
us roads to go,

is spirit without

which sun would go out
and every thought
and passion die;
it is time to break
the grip of the book
and, worshipping, look
on earth, sea, sky.

The Cyhydedd Hir pattern is:
    Syllables: 5 5 5 4
    End rhymes: A A A B
    The B rhyme is the final rhyming word of the following stanza.
A different B line is usually used for the following pair of stanzas.
The A rhyme alters from stanza to stanza. Occasionally two stanzas are presented as two rhyming lines of 19 syllables each, to create a single stanza, as in this example.

C Y H Y D E D D   N A W   B A N

S e a b o r n

In the weed-fringed pool I see my eyes
staring up at me with no surprise,
creatures of the sea's own paradise.
I'll remember this if I am wise;
visions from the deep are never lies;
dying, I will hear the gull's wild cries.

The Cyhydedd Naw Ban pattern is:
    Syllables: 9 9
    End rhymes: A A
    A stanza may be made up of several couplets, all using the same

endrhyme. There is no rule as to the number of couplets that should be combined in this manner.

Westfield Lane Revisited

Riding down time's grassy lane
I was never quite alone;
always birds were skimming on
ahead of me; the overgrown
hedges clustering and green
that I cycled in between
made them arbours where they slid,
leaf-clad, and hid, were lost and gone.

Why do I recall those days?
Gazing here on dying grass
as the summer hungers pass
I can't say, but I suppose,
now the curtain starts to close
upon the evening light, I miss
boyhood journeys that were sure
joy would endure beyond all this.

The Cyrch A Chwta pattern:
    Syllables: 7 7 7 7 7 7 7 7
    End rhymes: A A A A A A B A
    The A words may either rhyme or consonate or both. The B word rhymes with A word in the middle of the line following.

Carillon

Do not presume
his little room
too small to hold
those bells of gold
that peal the true
heart-haunting due
of she that wakes
the song and makes
the tune correct,
nor, please, reject
my keeping time
with narrow rhyme
as game or guile:
these verses, while
they may be short
are wrought to court
her loving will
by calling skill
to play its part
with head and heart
in forging here
for my true dear,
and for none else,
twelve chiming bells.

The Cywydd Deuair Firion pattern is:
   Syllables: 4 4
   End rhymes: A A
   A number of couplets using the same rhyme may be combined
to form a stanza or poem; these may also be composed of a number
of couplets using different rhymes.

That Evening

My dear, do you remember
how in the chill evening air

for all the winds' complaining
we blessed what the night would bring?

My dear, do you remember
how in the red sunset there

we granted the hurt sky's want
and fashioned love's covenant?

The Cywydd Deuair Hirion pattern is:
    Syllables: 7 7
    End rhymes: A A
    One of the end rhymes is stressed and one unstressed; it does
not matter in what order. The couplets may be combined to form a
poem or stanza or may be regarded as separate stanzas.

Speechless

following the pattern of Cystudd y Bardd by Dafyd ap Gwilym.

Words are almost wholly gone.
When I crave communion,

ways to make thought register,
wantonly words won't appear,
will not answer knock or ring
wearing smiles and carrying
whispered syllables that bless
worried heads with gentleness,
wise old saying, broken, bent,
worn out by reargument,
wary fables of man's fall
woven from the mystical,
wild yarns rank with rhetoric,
worthy volumes for the sick,
wedding hymns and rhymes for kids
welcome, all. The question is
what will help me to recall,
waking the subliminal,
wondrous verbs and splendid nouns,
wily clauses, semi-colons
working busily to get
witty verse or verselet,
watchful syntax, wearying,
waiting for them all to bring
wealth of meaning it may share
with some shrewd interpreter?
"Why do I feel damned?" I cry.
Wisdom answers quietly
with a truth Yeats understood,
"Words alone are certain good."

In this invention the lines all begin with the same sound.

Dimlington Heights

In Memoriam William Robins

Here on the cliff edge, staring down
upon the hard-packed sand, the brown
slabs of pounded boulder clay,
I think how Grandfather would ride
his pony trap out where the tide
has hidden his fields away.

There was a fine old farm out there
more than a mile off shore, but where
exactly no one dare say;
does it bulk whole beneath the sea,
a stone house for eternity,
or has it been swept away?

What we remember has not gone,
although, because we scurry on
without a stop or stay
we think what's gone is gone for good,
the past stands where it's always stood;
it never could move away

for it's our heart, our head, our hand,
the very substance of the land,
each thought, each word we've said,
and that house drowned beneath the tide
has dark rooms that we hunt inside
for a guide to ride ahead.

The Cywydd Llosgyrnog pattern is:
Syllables: 8 8 7 8 8 7
End rhymes: A A B C C B
Endword A rhymes with a word in the middle of the third line.
Endword c rhymes with a word in the middle of line six.

E N G L Y N   B Y R   C W C A

Full Moon

Seeing pallid moonlit stones
beside the tide I feel Time's died and bow
down to the earth's cold bones.

The Englyn Byr Cwca pattern is:
Syllables: 7 10 6
End rhymes: A   B   A
The B end word rhymes with a word or syllable in the third line,
frequently in the middle of it.

E N G L Y N   C Y R C H

The Cliff

For Michael Seward Snow

Staring here upon the face
of this steep clay cliff I trace

fragments of lost centuries,
past histories of a place

that changed shape age by age.
A scholarly mind might gauge
how, when and why, but I
won't meddle with that dry page,

for I sense there's something more.
I see it as a closed door,
fast bolted, a word unsaid,
and am led to think a law

controls all the games we play
with time and the mortal clay,
a law about man-made fate.
I'd wait my days away

If I could be sure I'd find
that fast-shut door in the mind
open and comprehend
what end is planned for mankind,

but that vast expanse of clay
has nothing that it may say.
We're living and then we die,
forgetful. I turn away.

The Englyn Cyrch pattern is:
    Syllables: 7 7 7 7
    End rhymes: A A B A
    The endword B rhymes into the middle of the fourth line.

In Boyhood

At the edge of Blashill's field
ran a deep ditch, narrow, cold;
I squatted there as a child
with twigs I gathered and sailed.

The launching of boats appealed
for I had read and been told
of islands and reefs and wild
storms when the high winds wailed.

And the quick brown water healed
a hurt in me; I was old
in loneliness, felt exiled
somehow, and the world had staled.

But there as I gathered, kneeled,
and launched my ships, grown bold
with future journeys, I smiled;
those distances never failed.

The Englyn Lleddfbroest pattern is:
   Syllables 7 7 7 7
   In Welsh, the end words of each stanza carry the four Welsh dipthongs which do not exist in English. Each stanza presents these dipthongs, not necessarily in the same order. An English version can only imitate the use of dipthongs in an approximate fashion.

Love's Wisdom

The time of doubt is over:
I seek now to recover
the wisdom of the lover

who has the sacred power
to be in every hour
at once root, fruit, and flower,

ocean and river and brook
and fountaining spring, and look
through every secret book

as if through lens of crystal,
finding the paradisal,
and think it no miracle.

The Englyn Milwr pattern is:
    Syllables: 7 7 7
    End rhymes: A A A

The Hearing

*Following the pattern of the anonymous fourteenth century
poem Englynion y Clyweit (Stanzas of Hearing)*

Lover, have you learned to hear,
whispered in the secret ear,
Love is all that love should fear?

Have you heard the blackbird sing,
lifting up its burnished wing,
Love is darkness quarrelling?

Have you listened to the sound
of the night owl on its round,
Love is what the vole has found?

Have you heard at end of night
rafters creakingly recite,
Love is burdened by the light?

Have you woken to the spell
rising from the moss-coped well,
Love is Heaven kissing Hell?

Have you turned your head to hear
from the grasses on the weir,
Love is far, but Death is near?

Has the sudden trodden stone
greeted you with helpless moan,
Love must mourn and lie alone?

Have you heard the plover cry
from the ploughland to the sky,
Love is cloud run careless by?

Have you listened to the snail
chaining leaf with silver trail,
Love is beak and Love is nail?

Have you, tossing in your sheet,
heard the whisper at your feet,
Love is but a garnished meat?

Have you heard within the wave
rearing from the seaman's grave,
Love will drown what Love would save?

Yet, for all this, have you heard
with each dark and warning word,
Love is what God's finger stirred?

ENGLYN PENFYR

May Day

On this early May morning, chill and dry,
larks high over the hill,
I sense no impending ill.

Yet May has a dangerous charm; it brings
yearnings that haunt and harm
against which nobody can arm.

Love may prove a beautiful cheat, a ruse,
choosing to feed earth's heat,
giving it our bones to eat.

The Englyn Penfyr pattern is:
    Syllables: 10 7 7
    End rhymes: A   A   A
    The first A word occurs before the end of the first line, and the
one, two or three syllables that follow it are echoed in the first
syllables of the line following.

ENGLYN   PROEST   DALGRON

All

Whether she be far or near,
she is all that I desire,
moving through the midnight hour
to a heaven-haunted air

that, awakening the heart,
chokes with tears the burning throat,
stealing through the lonely night,
reaffirming mortal fate

with a song that, searing, proves
man, though murdered if he loves,
must lie nameless if he leaves
love no cause to grieve his graves.

The Englyn Proest Dalgron pattern is:

Syllables: 7 7 7 7
End rhymes: A A A A

The endrhymes are all near-rhymes, each one having a slightly different vowel or dipthong. All the end words are the same as regards to the stress they possess and their "quantity" which is to say the length of the vowel sounds and the consonants.

ENGLYN PROEST GADWYNOG

Somnium

These nights when I fall asleep
I dream strangely and reshape
memories I'd like to keep,
but they alter, step by step.

I spent half my life in dream,
hardly even knew my name,
only knew that things that seem
never seem a second time.

So perhaps I should not care,
should not call my dream a liar,
if I'm altered here and there,
less grown less and more grown more.

Transformation is Time's game
played within a shifting stream
of air and water, earth and flame;
dream is how we learn our home.

The Englyn proest Gadwynog:
Syllables: 7 7 7 7
End rhymes: A B A C
The B and C end words off-rhyme with each other and with A.
The off-rhyme may take the form of a pararhyme or, less rigor-
ously, of consonance.

ENGLYN UNODL CRWCA

Humberside, 1939

Beyond the end of the lane
the Humber lay like a stain
of brown on the green stretched plain and there I'd
ride again and again.

possessed by the edge of things,
the end of all wanderings
spread under the crying wings of the gulls,
drowned souls from voyagings

long past, or so I was told;
joining the river, I rolled
up my pants and, bare toed, strolled in the mud
skin-chilling, clinging, cold,

black, oozy, soft; it was said
the blood of the Celts ran red
in this estuary bed and, alone
with death, I turned my head

and stared out where Spurn Light
stood on its hillock, white

against grey heaven, poised nightlong to keep
our sleep secure; there might,

they said, be another war,
across on the low far shore
of Lincolnshire were there more like me
who had been here before?

The Englyn Unodl Crwca pattern is:
    Syllables: 7 7 10 6
    End rhymes: A A A A
The A word in line 3 occurs before the end of the line and the
one, two or three syllables that follow it are echoed in the first
syllables of the line following.

ENGLYN UNODL UNION

Fulfillments

When snowdrops nod white under grey-lit skies
making time seem tender,
we sense the end of winter,
the whole world rapt with wonder.

When blossoms begin to fall and lightly,
brightly, stain and shawl
the crown of the orchard wall,
Spring is done and Summer's all.

When one ripe apple nods upon the high
skied bough and mimes the sun
Summer's race is almost run;
blessings fall on everyone.

The Englyn Unodl Union pattern is:

Syllables: 10 6 7 7
End rhymes: A A A A

As in other formulae the A word in the longest line occurs before the end and the syllables following it are echoed in the beginning of the line following.

G W A W D O D Y N

Clair de Lune

Slowly clouds unveil the riding moon;
branches curve up high as if they mean
somehow to celebrate the scene, to bless
the peace the Goddess brings to Her demesne.

Leaning lonely on the garden gate,
watching a smooth bough stir, I pray some fate
will bring me soon the light that's Hers alone
and that trees have long known. I wait. I wait.

The Gwawdodyn pattern is:

Syllables: 9 9 10 9
End rhymes: A A B A

The B rhyme may link with A B word in the same line, or if it occurs before the actual end of the line, it may rhyme into the middle of the line following.

Ammunition Nation

It is the ordinary appalls,
the commonplaces, — towering walls,
barred windows, tall and searchlit towers,
the uniforms in markets and in malls.

It is the day's reports that frighten —
the way death makes expressions brighten,
headlines and nooses tighten, cities fall,
hunger splinter ribs and new bones whiten.

It is this universe terrifies;
we have thrown away both truths and lies
and only prize the maggot in the head
that burrows till we cannot hear men's cries.

The Gwawdodyn Byr pattern is:
    Syllables: 9 9 10 10
    End rhymes: A A B A
    A word in the middle of the third line rhymes with A.

Shore Birds

Brushing through coarse grasses of the dunes,
wondering, I stare at tiny bones

white upon white sand, the frail remains
of birds; pale eggs like little rounded stones
have hatched here in the sun-warm scooped-out sand
and somewhere round about there should be terns.

There are none. I walk the wave-ribbed sand
considering the creatures no one's found,
legends, monsters, myths of sea and land,
phoenix, unicorn, and in my mind
these words resound: All freedom is unseen
and it has been and will be till the end.

The Gwawdodyn Hir pattern is:
    Syllables: 9 9 9 9 10 10
    End rhymes: A A A A B A
    The B word may, if it occurs before the end of the line, rhyme
into the middle of the line following, or it may rhyme with a word
presented earlier in the same line.

Hir A Thoddaid

Stone Music

For Myfanwy Pavelic

Down on the shore I held a shining stone —
shining because a veil of spray had blown
upon its sea-smoothed form — and once again
I heard a harmony, tides' undertone,
a singing ripple in the bone; my hand
was filled with sounds of silences I'd known.

Hands that may never tease the keys or strings
may yet have hidden repertoires of songs
uncovered in the rough and smooth of things;
the grains of wood, the feather's curve, the cling
of silks, fur's warmth, are all undying airs;
our fingers share in their awakenings.

Music is not peculiar to the ear;
it may be soundless as now on this shore
bright stones swept up from the dark ocean floor
create still silent harmonies that soar
beyond our skills to score, for none may own
a shining stone or close light's open door.

The Hir A Thoddaid pattern is:
    Syllables: 10 10 10 10 10 10
    End rhymes: A A A A B A
The seventh, eighth or ninth syllable in the fifth line rhymes
with the A words. The B word rhymes into the middle of the sixth
line.

R H U P U N T _____

The Mark

When I began
I was a man
released by dark,

then, given sight,
worked in the light
to make my mark,

which fades away
day by worn day
for all my sweat

that I may learn
I must return
and will forget.

The Rhupunt pattern is:
   Syllables: 4 4 4
   End rhymes: A A B
   Stanzas may be of three, four or five lines, the last line rhyming
with the last line of the stanza following. The lines are regarded as
being sections of a long line and may be presented as such, in which
case one could regard the Rhupunt as a couplet with lines of twelve
to twenty syllables.

LONG RHUPUNT

The Knowledge

I think I know
the wind although
I cannot show
the leaf its dance.

I think I know
the stream although
I only flow
from chance to chance.

I understand,

I think, earth, land,
although my hand
cannot make clay.

I sense in fire
this world's desire
though from time's pyre
ash blows away.

And you who are
tide, burning star,
clear air and far
earth's deep also

I think I know
by heart, although
I cannot show
the love I owe.

The Long Rhupunt has four parts to the line or (as presented here) the stanza, each part being of four syllables and the lines rhyming A A A B, with the B rhyme ending the line (or stanza) immediately following. The Long Rhupunt, with the two lines (or stanzas) run together was a not uncommon English lyric form in the Tudor period, and can be found in Wyatt.

Ars Longa

Love is a skill
I slowly learn
as long years turn
my dry hair white

and passions chill
and scar and burn
for I discern
each day, each night,

another lack,
another way
in which I play
the music false;

the strings go slack,
the hands astray:
perhaps none may
command the pulse

to perfect art
and poise, and yet
I think to get
one flawless air

before my heart
disdain the fret
and, old, forget
eyes, lips, breasts, hair.

The Tawddgyrch Cadwynog pattern is:
    Syllables: 4 4 4 4
    End rhymes: A B B C
The A word rhymes with the first line of the following stanza and the C word with the last line. Thus the stanzas must be composed in pairs.

T O D D A I D

On the Mountain

Those who have met her on the mountain swear
that no account of her can ring true
to ears that once have heard the fir-tree sigh
and shudder of her speech renew

each fretted crystal of the long-smirched snow;
those who have seen, who have touched her, swear
that, though they ache, they never can return,
having taken such wild oaths to her

as none, and certainly not they, might keep,
binding them so tight by heart and hand
they are all foresworn and must forever
moil and mourn their green low-lying land.

The Toddaid pattern is:
    Syllables: 10 9 10 9
    End rhymes: A B   C   B
A syllable near the end of the first line rhymes with a syllable in the middle of the second line, and the same rhyming occurs between lines three and four.

YIDDISH

Night Walk

Rain black on the night road
under the yellow lamplight
seems almost a kind of mirror
offering us all foresight,

a glimpse of the far dark future
surrounding the shape-changing shadows
we cast as we stroll, not thinking about
the ways of inevitable tomorrows,

though if we stop, look down, stare,
something looks back at us;
what nightwalker can bear to see
his own eyes as ominous.

This is a podic metre; each line has four stressed syllables and the
number of unstressed syllables is not considered. The rhyme scheme
is A B C B. This is a nineteenth century stanza.

West Coast December

Grey days, bare trees,
black-brown sodden leaves
trampled in grass, snow berries
emptily nodding; winter leaves

little but hope for the weary hours
to hold as the darkness drifts down
earlier, earlier, and heavy showers
drum, drum through the dusk of noon.

There are four stressed syllables in each line of verse and the rhyme scheme is A B A B. This is a form of the nineteenth century.

Concluding

The loud sunset spells
an end to day's triumphs and debacles,
drawing a crimson theatrical curtain
across the stage on which we have taken part
in actions we have been told are truth and art;
of the next dark act we are uncertain.

Each line has four stressed syllables and an uncounted number of unstressed ones. The rhyme scheme is A A B C C B.